Granville Sharp, John Adams

The Just Limitation of Slavery in the Laws of God

Compared With the Unbounded Claims of the African Traders and British American

Slaveholders

Granville Sharp, John Adams

The Just Limitation of Slavery in the Laws of God
Compared With the Unbounded Claims of the African Traders and British American Slaveholders

ISBN/EAN: 9783744794541

Printed in Europe, USA, Canada, Australia, Japan

Cover: Foto ©ninafisch / pixelio.de

More available books at **www.hansebooks.com**

THE

JUST LIMITATION OF SLAVERY

IN THE

LAWS OF GOD,

COMPARED WITH

The unbounded Claims of the AFRICAN TRADERS and BRITISH AMERICAN SLAVEHOLDERS.

BY GRANVILLE SHARP.

With a copious APPENDIX:

CONTAINING,

An Anſwer to the Rev. Mr. Thompſon's Tract in favour of the *African Slave Trade.*—Letters concerning *the lineal Deſcent of the Negroes* from the Sons of HAM.—The Spaniſh Regulations for the gradual Enfranchiſement of Slaves.—A Propoſal on the ſame Principles for the gradual Enfranchiſement of Slaves in *America.*—Reports of Determinations in the ſeveral COURTS OF LAW AGAINST SLAVERY, &c.

----Take away your Exactions from my People, SAITH THE LORD GOD! Ezekiel xlv. 9.

LONDON:

Printed for B. WHITE, in Fleet-Street, and E. and C. DILLY, in the Poultry.

M.DCC.LXXVI.

TRACT I.

THE

Juſt Limitation of Slavery.

THE opinion of the lords Hardwick and Talbot, which I laboured to refute in my Tract againſt *Slavery in England* (1), (printed in 1769,) has ſince been effectually ſet aſide by a clear determination, in the Court of King's-Bench (2), in favour of *James Somerſett, a Negro*, againſt his former Maſter, C****** S******, eſq. in the year 1772.

But

---

(1) A Repreſentation of the Injuſtice and dangerous Tendency of tolerating Slavery in *England*.

(2) See Appendix.

But it is not enough, that the Laws of England exclude *Slavery* merely *from this ifland*, whilft the grand Enemy of mankind triumphs in a toleration, *throughout our Colonies*, of the moft monftrous *oppreffion* to which human nature can be fubjected!

And yet this abominable wickednefs has not wanted advocates, who, in a variety of late publications, have attempted to palliate the guilt, and have even ventured to appeal to Scripture for the fupport of their uncharitable pretenfions: fo that I am laid under a double obligation to anfwer them, becaufe it is not the caufe of *Liberty* alone for which I now contend, but for that which I have ftill much more at heart, the honour of the holy Scriptures, the principles of which are entirely oppofite to the felfifh and uncharitable

uncharitable pretenſions of our American Slaveholders and African Traders.

A late anonymous writer, who calls himſelf "*An African Merchant*," remarks, that,—" By the Law of Moſes, " the Iſraelites might purchaſe Slaves " from the Heathens, and even their " own people might become Slaves to " their brethren." *A Treatiſe on the Trade from Great-Britain to Africa, &c. by an African Merchant.* P. 8 *and* 9.

Now, with reſpect to the firſt part of his obſervation, it is true, indeed, that the Iſraelites were expreſſly permitted to keep Bond-Servants, or Slaves; " of the " *Heathen*, (or, more properly, of the " *Nations* הגוים) that *were round about*" *them*, and of " the children of the ſtran- " gers that ſojourned among" them. (Levit. xxv. 44 to 46.) But we muſt remember, that theſe *Heathen*, or " *Na-*
" *tions*

" *tions that were round about them,*" were an abandoned race of people, already *Slaves* and *worshippers* of devils, and by them led to debase *human nature*, and to pollute themselves with the most unnatural and abominable vices: " For in " all these," (said the Almighty,) " the " nations are defiled which I cast out " before you: and the Land is defiled; " THEREFORE I do visit the iniquity " thereof upon it, and the land itself vo- " miteth out her inhabitants," &c. Again: " For all these abominations have " the men of the land done which " were before you, and the land is defi- " led," &c. See Levit. xviii. And the " *children of the strangers,*" abovementioned, were (probably) also of the same detestable nations of Palestine, the Amorites, Canaanites, &c. which were expressly doomed to destruction (3), and that

---

(3) " Observe thou that which I command thee
" this day: behold, I drive out before thee the Amo-
" rite,

that by the hand of the Ifraelites, *who were commanded to ſhew them no pity* (4).

But no doctrine muſt be drawn from theſe commands to *execute God's vengeance* upon the ſaid wicked *ſtrangers*, without conſidering, at the ſame time, *that very contrary treatment of ſtrangers* which was *equally* enjoined in the Law: for the Ifraelites were poſitively commanded not to *vex* or *oppreſs a Stranger.* " *Thou*
" *ſhalt*

" rite, and the Canaanite, and the Hittite, and the
" Perizzite, and the Hivite, and the Jebuſite. Take
" heed to thyſelf, leſt thou make a covenant with the
" inhabitants of the land whither thou goeſt, leſt it be
" for a ſnare in the midſt of thee," &c. Exod. xxxiv.
11 and 12.

(4) " And thou ſhalt conſume all the people which
" the Lord thy God ſhall deliver thee: thine eye ſhall
" have *no pity upon them*," &c. Deut. vii. 16. " The
" Lord thy God will put out thoſe nations by little and
" little," &c. " The Lord thy God ſhall deliver
" them unto thee, and ſhall deſtroy them with a migh-
" ty deſtruction until they be deſtroyed. And he ſhall
" deliver their kings into thine hand, and thou ſhalt
" deſtroy their name from under heaven: there ſhall
" no man be able to ſtand before thee until thou have
" deſtroyed them." Deut. vii. 23 and 24.

"*shalt love him as thyself,*" said Moses, by the express command of God. "If a Stranger sojourn with thee in your land, ye *shall not vex*" (or *oppress*) him. But *the Stranger* that dwelleth with you shall be unto you as one born among you, and *thou shalt love him as thyself*: for ye were *Strangers* in the land of Egypt." Levit. xix. 33. 34. And again: "The Lord your God is God of gods and Lord of lords, a great God, a mighty and a terrible, which *regardeth not persons* nor taketh reward: he doth execute the judgement of the fatherless and widow, and *loveth the Stranger*, in giving him food and raiment. *Love ye*, therefore, *the Stranger*; for ye *were Strangers* in the land of Egypt." Deut. x. 17 to 19. In all these passages, and many others, the Israelites were reminded of their *Bondage in Egypt*: for so the almighty *Deliverer* from *Slavery* warned his people

to

to *limit* and moderate the *bondage*, which the Law permitted, by the remembrance of *their own former bondage* in a foreign land, and by a remembrance alfo of his great mercy *in delivering them* from that *bondage*: and he exprefsly referred them to *their own feelings*, as they themfelves had experienced the intolerable yoke of Egyptian Tyranny! " Thou fhalt not " *opprefs a Stranger*; for ye know the " heart of *a ftranger*, feeing ye were " *ftrangers* in the land of Egypt." Exod. xxiii. 9. And again: " Thou fhalt " remember that *thou* waft *a Bond-man* " in the land of Egypt, and the Lord thy " God *redeemed thee*:" Deut. xv. 15.

We muft, therefore, necefsarily conclude, when thefe very oppofite commands are confidered, that the *Heathen*, or *nations* that were " ROUND ABOUT," or in the *environs* of the promifed land, and alfo the *children of the ftrangers*, that
dwelt

dwelt among them, mentioned at the same time, whom the Israelites were permitted to retain *in perpetual bondage*, were not intended to be included and ranked under that general denomination of *Strangers*, to whom so much real *affection, benevolence,* and *consideration*, are strictly commanded, in the texts to which I have just now referred. And, consequently, it must be allowed, that the particular nations, (the seven nations of Palestine, see Deut. vii. 1.) which were expressly devoted to destruction, were the only *Strangers* whom the Jews were permitted to hold in *absolute Slavery*; so that the wicked practice of *enslaving* the poor *African Negroes* would have been as *unlawful*, under the Jewish Dispensation, as it certainly is, now a-days, to Englishmen, and other subjects of Great-Britain, that profess *the Christian Religion*; *in whose consideration*, ALL STRANGERS, from every other

other part of the world, are, without doubt, entitled to be ranked, efteemed, and beloved, *as brethren*, which I have elfewhere particularly demonftrated; and which even the law of Mofes exprefsly commanded:—" But *the ftranger*, that
" dwelleth with you, fhall be unto you *as*
" *one born among you*, and THOU
" SHALT LOVE HIM AS THY-
" SELF; for *ye were ftrangers* in the
" land of Egypt: I am the Lord your
" God." Levit. xix. 33 and 34.

This excellent fyftem of benevolence to *ftrangers*, which the Ifraelites were fo ftrictly enjoined to obferve, cannot, I apprehend, be otherwife reconciled with the permiffion to the Ifraelites of retaining in perpetual bondage *the heathen that were round about them*, and the children of *the ftrangers* that fojourned among them: for, if this permiffion were to be extended to *ftrangers in general*, it would

C fubvert

subvert the express command concerning *brotherly love* due to *strangers*; because a man cannot be said *to love the stranger as himself* if he holds *the stranger* and his progeny in a perpetual *involuntary servitude*. The observation therefore of the African Merchant, that " THE ISRAELITES *might* " *purchase Slaves from the heathens*," will by no means justify the *enslaving* of *modern heathens*, by *Englishmen*, or by any other nation now subsisting. The Israelites, at that time, might not only purchase Slaves of those particular heathen nations, but they might also *drive out these heathen*; (I mean, these which were particularly named;) nay, even *kill* (5) and *extirpate* them, and *take possession of their cities, houses*, and *lands*. All these acts of violence *might* the Israelites do *without sin*, though the like would justly be esteemed
murder

(5) " But of the cities of these people, which the
" Lord thy God doth give thee for an inheritance,
" thou *shalt save alive nothing that breatheth*." Deut.
xx. 16.

murder and *robbery*, if practised by any other nation, not under the like peculiar circumstances: so that the example of the Israelites affords no excuse for the uncharitable practices of the *African Merchant* and *West-India Planter!* The Israelites had an express commission (6) to execute God's vengeance, *without remorse* (7), upon several populous nations, which had rendered themselves *abominable in the sight of God*,

(6) " Now, therefore, kill every male among the " little ones, and kill every woman that hath known " man by lying with him." Numbers xxxi. 17. This was the judgement against the Midianitish prisoners. The seven nations of Palestine were likewise subjected to the same condemnation. " Thou shalt smite them " and utterly destroy them: thou shalt make no cove- " nant with them, *nor shew mercy unto them.*" Deut. vii. 2. And a reason for this condemnation was plainly delivered in the fourth verse, to confirm the justice of it: " For they will turn away thy son from follow- " ing me, that they may serve other gods."

The Amalekites were also doomed to destruction in the like manner: " Thou shalt *blot out the remembrance* " *of Amalek from under heaven; thou shalt not forget it.* Deut. xxv. 19.

(7) " And thou shalt *consume all the people* which " the Lord thy God shall deliver thee; thine eye " shall have *no pity* upon them. Deut. vii. 16.

God, and therefore deserved no consideration; so that *even mercy*, in the Israelites, was a sin (8), when it interfered with this positive command of God!

The commission there given, however, was but *temporary*; and no other nation, except

(8) "But, if ye will not drive out the inhabitants of the
" land from before you, then it shall come to pass, that
" those, which ye let remain of them, shall be pricks in
" your eyes and thorns in your sides, and shall vex you
" in the land wherein ye dwell. Moreover, it shall
" come to pass, that *I shall do unto you* as *I thought to do*
" *unto them*." Numb. xxxiii. 55 and 56. And the Israelites were expressly told, that it was not on their own account that this extraordinary authority was put into their hands, but on account of the *abominable wickedness* of those who possessed the promised land.—"The
" land is defiled; therefore I do visit *the iniquity there-*
" *of upon it, and the land itself vomiteth out her inhabit-*
" *ants.*" Levit. xviii. 25.

" For all these abominations" (unnatural lusts, mentioned in the former part of the same chapter)
" have the men of the land done which were before
" you; and the land is defiled." Levit. xviii. 27. And the Israelites were warned against presumption, lest such extraordinary authority should occasion spiritual pride.
" Not for thy righteousness, or for the uprightness of
" thine heart, *dost thou* go to possess the land, but for
" *the wickedness of those nations the Lord God doth drive*
" *them out from before thee,*" &c. Deut. ix. 5.

except God's peculiar people, was charged with the execution of it; and therefore, though the Europeans have taken upon themselves, for a long time past, *to attack, destroy, drive out, dispossess, and enslave*, the poor ignorant *Heathen*, in many distant parts of the world, and may, perhaps, plead custom and prescription (to their shame be it said) for their actions, yet, as they cannot, like the Israelites, produce an *authentic written commandment from God* for such proceedings, the offenders can no otherwise be esteemed than as *lawless robbers* and *oppressors*, who have reason to expect *a severe retribution* from God for their tyranny and oppression. It is unreasonable, therefore, to suppose that the severe treatment of the *ancient Heathen*, by the Israelites, under *the dispensation of the Law*, either in *killing, dispossessing,* or *enslaving,* them, should justify our *modern* acts of *violence*

violence and *oppression*, now that we profess obedience to the *Gospel of Peace*.

And, with respect to the second part of the African Merchant's observation, concerning the Israelites, (*viz.* that even " their own people might become Slaves " to their brethren,") I must remark, that he does not deal fairly by the Jewish Law, to quote that circumstance, without mentioning, at the same time, "*the* " *Just Limitation*" to which it was subject, and the admirable provision, in the same Law, against *the involuntary servitude of brethren*; because no Hebrew could be made *a Slave* without *his own consent*, and even *desire*, which was to be " *plainly*" and *openly* declared in a court of *record* : — " if the servant shall *plainly* " *say*, I love my master, my wife, and " my children, *I will not go out free*, then" (says the text) " his master shall bring " him *unto the Judges*," &c. (whereby

an

an acknowledgement *in a court of record* is plainly implied,) " and his master
" shall bore his ear through with an aul;
" and he shall serve him for ever." Exod.
xxi. 5. 6. But, without that *public acknowledgement* of *voluntary consent before the Judges*, the Hebrew master had no authority to bore the servant's ear (9) in token of bondage: and, in every other case, it was *absolutely unlawful* for the Israelite to hold a *Brother Israelite in Slavery!* The Law expressly declares, " If
" thy *Brother*, (*that dwelleth*) by thee, be
" waxen poor, and *be sold unto thee*; *thou*
" *shalt not* compel him to serve as a *bond*
" *servant: (but)* as an *hired servant*;
" and

(9) Yet our inconsiderate West-Indian and American Planters make no scruple even of *branding* their poor Negro-servants with a *hot iron*, to mark them *for perpetual Bondmen, against their will*, though they are certainly their *Brethren* in the eyes of GOD. But GOD hath declared, *expressly*, concerning the crimes of these men, *who enslave the poor*, —— " SURELY, *I will ne-*
" *ver forget any of their works! Shall not the land trem-*
" *ble for this!*" &c.! &c.! &c.! Amos, viii. 7. 8. See also the whole context, from the 4th verse.

" and as a *sojourner* he shall be with
" thee; *(and)* shall serve thee unto the
" year of jubilee: and *(then)* shall he
" depart from thee, *(both)* he *and his chil-
" dren* with him;" &c. (and the reason
of this command immediately follows;)
" for they are *my servants*," (said the
Lord,) " which I brought forth out of
" the land of Egypt:" (i. e. *which God
himself delivered from Slavery:*) " they
" *shall not be sold as Bond-men*: thou shalt
" not rule over him with rigour, but
" *shalt fear thy God.*" Levit. xxv. 39
to 43. And again, in the 55th verse,
" For *unto me*" (said the Lord) " the
" children of *Israel are servants; they are
" my servants,* whom I brought out of
" the land of Egypt: *I am the Lord
" your God.*"

Thus it appears that the *involuntary
servitude* of *brethren* is entirely inconsistent with the Jewish Law; which, therefore,

fore, is so far from *justifying* the *African Merchant*, that it absolutely *condemns* him. But he is still more mistaken, when he insinuates that Slavery is not inconsistent with the Gospel. " Jesus Christ, the
" Saviour of mankind and Founder of
" our religion," (says he,) " left the
" moral laws and civil rights of mankind
" upon their old foundations: his king-
" dom was not of this world, nor did he
" interfere with national laws: *he did*
" *not repeal that of slaves*, nor assert an
" universal freedom, except from sin:
" with him bond and free were accepted,
" if they behaved *righteously*." &c. p. 9.

But how can a man be said to " behave
" *righteously*," who sells his *brethren*, or holds them in Slavery *against their will?* For, though, with Christ, " *bond* and *free*
" are accepted," yet it behoves *the African Merchant* very diligently to examine, whether he is not likely to forfeit his *own*

D *acceptance*,

acceptance, if he does not moſt heartily repent of having *enſlaved his brethren,* and of having encouraged others to the ſame *uncharitable practices,* by miſinterpreting the holy Scriptures.

Under the Goſpel Diſpenſation, *all mankind* are to be eſteemed *our brethren.* Chriſt commanded his diſciples to go and teach (or make diſciples of) *all nations,* " παντα τα εθνη." Matth. xxviii. 19. So that *men of all nations* (who, indeed, were *brethren* before, by *natural* deſcent from *one common father*) are now, undoubtedly, capable of being doubly related to us, by a *farther* tie of *of brotherhood,* which the law of Moſes ſeemed to deny them, and of which the peculiar people of God (jealous of their own adoption) once thought them incapable; I mean, the ineſtimable privilege of becoming ſons, alſo, to *one almighty Father, by adoption,* as well as the Jews, and, conſequently, of being

being *our brethren*, through Chrift, by a *fpiritual*, as well as a *natural*, relation-fhip.

The promifes of God, likewife, in every other part of the New Teftament, are made to *all mankind in general, without exception*; fo that a Negro, as well as any other man, is capable of becoming " *an adopted fon of God*;" an " *heir of God* " *through Chrift*" (10); a " *temple of the* " *Holy-Ghoft*" (11); " *an heir* (12) *of*
" *falva-*

(10)—" that we might receive the *adoption of* Sons." (faid the apoftle, to the Galatians:) " And, becaufe " *ye are Sons*, God hath fent forth the fpirit of *his Son* " into your hearts, crying *Abba, Father*: wherefore " thou art *no more a fervant, but a* Son; and, *if a Son*, " then AN HEIR OF GOD THROUGH CHRIST." Galat. iv. 5. 6. and 7.

(11) " Know ye not that ye are the Temple of " God, and that the Spirit of God dwelleth in you? " If any man defile the temple of God, him fhall God " deftroy; for the *Temple* of God *is holy*, which *Temple ye are*." 1 Corinth. iii. 16. 17. See alfo chap. vi. 19. 20.

(12) " That the Gentiles fhould be *fellow-heirs*, " and of the fame body, and partakers of his promife " in Chrift *by the Gofpel*." Ephef. iii. 6.

" *salvation;*" a partaker of *the divine nature* (13); " a *joint-heir with Christ* (14); and capable, also, of being joined to that glorious company of Saints, who shall one day " *come with him to judge the world;*" for " the *Saints shall judge the world.*" 1 Cor. vi. 2. 3. — And, therefore, how can any man, who calls himself a Christian, presume to retain, as a mere chattel, or *private property*, his fellow man and *brother*, who is equally capable with himself of attaining the high dignities abovementioned! Let Slaveholders be mindful of the approaching consummation of all earthly things, when, perhaps, they will see thousands of those men, who were formerly esteemed mere *chattels*

(13) — " through the knowledge of him that hath
" called us to *glory* and *virtue*: whereby are given unto
" us exceeding great and precious promises; that by
" these ye might *be partakers* of the *divine nature.*"
&c. 2 Pet. i. 3 and 4.

(14) " If children, then heirs; heirs of God and
" joint-heirs with Christ:" &c. Rom. viii. 17.

tels and *private property*, coming (15) in the clouds (16), with their heavenly Master, to judge tyrants and oppressors, and to call them to account for their want of *brotherly love!*

The Ethiopians, or Negroes, received the Christian faith *much sooner* than the Europeans themselves: their *early* conversion was foretold by the Psalmist: (Psalm

(15) — " at the *coming* of our Lord JESUS CHRIST " *with all his Saints.*" 1 Thess. iii. 13.

— " And Enoch also, the seventh from Adam, pro-
" phesied of these, saying, Behold, the Lord *cometh*,
" with *ten thousands of his saints, to execute judgement upon*
" *all*, and to convince all that are ungodly among them,
" of all their ungodly deeds," &c. Jude, xiv. 15.

(16) — " and then shall all the tribes of the earth
" mourn, and they shall see the Son of man coming in
" the clouds of heaven, with power and great glory."
Matt. xxiv. 30.

" Behold, he cometh with clouds, and every eye
" shall see him : and they also *which pierced him:*"
Rev. i. 7. And those men, also, who have worn out their brethren in slavery, may surely be ranked with the wretches that *pierced their Lord*. " — in as much as ye
" have done it *unto one of the least of these my brethren,*"
(said our Lord,) " *ye have done it unto me.*" Matt. xxv. 40. (See the conclusion of my Tract on the Law of Liberty.)

(Pſalm lxviii. 31.) " Princes ſhall come " out of Egypt," (or from *Mizraim*) ; " and Ethiopia" (17) (or *Cuſh*) " ſhall " ſoon ſtretch out her hands unto God." And, accordingly, we find the *Ethiopian* Eunuch (18) particularly mentioned in Scripture among the firſt converts to Chriſtianity:

(17) Wherever we find mention made, in the Old Teſtament, of *Ethiopians*, (though a general name for Negroes,) yet we ſhall find them expreſſed, in the Hebrew, by the name of the eldeſt branch of Ham, *viz*. *Chus*, כוש. However, we muſt remember, that all Ethiopians are not *Cuſhites*. The prodigious army, of a million of *Ethiopians*, which was overthrown by Aſa, were not all deſcendants of *Chus*, though mentioned under the general name of כושים *Chuſim*, in 2 Chron. chap. xiv. for we read, in the 16th chap. 8th verſe, that part of that vaſt body were *Lubims*. " Were not " the *Ethiopians* and *Lubims*" (הכושים והלובים) " a huge hoſt?" ſaid the prophet Hanani, when he reminded Aſa of his former ſuccefs. The *Lubims*, or *Libyans*, were a great nation, from whom the internal part of Africa receives its name of *Libya*, and were deſcended from Mizraim, the ſecond ſon of Ham, who was alſo the father of the Egyptians.

(18) Who might juſtly be eſteemed *a Prince* of that country, being Δυναςης, *a Lord*, or one " *of great autho-* " *rity* under Candace, Queen of the Ethiopians, *who* " *had the charge of all her Treaſure*," &c.

Christianity: and that extraordinary exertion of the HOLY SPIRIT, in favour of the eunuch, was, perhaps, the foundation of the ancient Church of Habaſſinia (19), which, notwithſtanding all worldly diſadvantages, remains in ſome degree of *purity* to this day, as a laſting monument of *Chriſtianity among the ſons of Ham*, even in the moſt remote and inacceſſible part of Africa!(20)

Certain

(19) The learned Lutholf was of a different opinion, and ſuppoſed that the Habaſſinians were not converted till the time of Conſtantine the Great, about the year 330; and, though it is not clear whether this latter period was the time of their firſt converſion or not, yet, certain it is, that, ever ſince that time, they have maintained the Chriſtian faith, and the ſacramental inſtitutions of Chriſt, without yielding to the adulterations of the church of Rome, though the ſame were preſſed upon them with all the authority that one of their own Emperors could exert! Lutholf has given a full and clear account (printed in 1691) of theſe Chriſtian Negroes and their church, which ſeems to be reſerved, by the providence of God, as a *Witneſs* of the purity of his holy Religion: a *Witneſs* not leſs remarkable than the church of the Vaudois!

(20) They ſtill retain Water-Baptiſm and the holy Communion *in both kinds,* and drove out the Portugueſe

Jeſuits

" Certain it is, (fay the learned Affembly
" of Divines,) that Ethiopia, according
" to this unqueftionable prophecy,"
(Pfalms, lxviii. 31.) " was one of the
" firft kingdoms that was converted to
" the Chriftian faith; the occafion and
" means whereof we read of Acts viii.
" 27, 28." &c.

The progrefs of the truth muft have been very rapid in Africa, becaufe we read of a council of African and Numidian Bifhops, held at Carthage, fo early as the year of Chrift 215 (21); (though our Anglo-Saxon anceftors remained in the groffeft pagan darknefs near 400 years afterwards;) and, in the year 240, a council of 99 Bifhops was affembled at Lambefa,

Jefuits for attempting, by force, to pervert and corrupt thefe *primitive rites*.

(21) " Carthaginenfe 1. circa annum ccxv. fub A-
" grippino, epifcopo Carthaginenfi, ab *Africæ* et *Nu-*
" *midiæ* epifcopis, *de rebaptizandis hæreticis habitum.*"
Dr. Cave's Hift. Literaria, p. 99.

Lambefa, an *inland city of Africa*, on the confines of Biledulgerid, againſt Privatus Biſhop of Lambefa on a charge of Herefie. (22) The fourth Council of Carthage in the year 253 was held by 66 Biſhops, concerning the Baptifm of Infants. (23) And in the eighth Council at that place (anno 256) befides (24) Prieſts, Deacons and Laymen, there were prefent 87 Biſhops. In another council of Carthage, about the year 308, no lefs than 270 Biſhops of the Sect of the Donatiſts (25) were prefent; and in the year 394, at Baga, an inland City of Africa, 310 (26) Biſhops were collected together, though the
E   fame

---

(22) Dr. Cave's Hiſt. Literaria, p. 99. (23) Ibid.

(24) " Prefentes erant preter Préfbyteros, Diaconos maximamque plebis partem, Epifcopi lxxxvii, &c. See Dr. Cave's Hiſt. Literaria, p. 100. alſo Bohun's Geog. Dict. p. 219, under the word *Lambefa*.

(25) Dr. Cave's Hiſt. Lit. p. 222. (26) Ibid. p. 234.

fame was long before the converfion of the Englifh and Dutch, the great traders in *African flaves*; and though the Africans have, fince, lamentably fallen back into grofs ignorance, yet we muft not, on that account, look upon them in the fame light that the Jews did upon "*the children of the ftrangers,*" whom they were permitted to hold in flavery (Levit. xxv. 45.) becaufe we cannot do fo without becoming *ftrangers* ourfelves to *Chriftianity*; and haftening *our own apoftacy*, which feems already too near at hand. (27) We may lament

---

(27) The alarming increafe of infidelity, and the open declarations of Deifts, Arians, Socinians, and others, who deny the Divinity of Chrift, and of the Holy Ghoft, are lamentable proofs of the growing apoftacy! The African Church fell away by degrees in the fame manner, till it was totally loft in the moft barbarous ignorance, (except in Habeffinia) for even thofe Africans who are free from idolatry, and profefs to worfhip *the true God*, are, neverthelefs, enfnared and enflaved.

ment the fallen ſtate of our unhappy brethren, but we have *no commiſſion under*

enſlaved in the groſs errors of *Mahometaniſm,* to which a neglect of the neceſſary Faith in the *Divinity of Chriſt,* and of the *Holy Ghoſt,* has an apparent tendency! We have likewiſe a remarkable inſtance of *infidelity,* or at leaſt of a total neglect of Scripture authority and revelation, in the attempt of two late writers to prove that Negroes are " *an inferior ſpecies of men :*" but the learned Dr. *Beattie,* in his *Eſſay on Truth,* has fully refuted the inſinuations of Mr. *Hume,* the firſt broacher of that uncharitable doctrine, as well as Ariſtotle's futile attempt to juſtify *ſlavery* ; ſo that Mr. *Eſtwick*'s ſubſequent attempt, which was prompted only by the authority of Mr. *Hume,* needs no further confutation.
" That I may not be thought a blind admirer of anti-
" quity, (ſays Dr. Beattie) I would here crave the read-
" er's indulgence for one ſhort digreſſion more, in order
" to put him in mind of an important error in morals,
" inferred from partial and inaccurate experience, by
" no leſs a perſon than Ariſtotle himſelf. He ar-
" gues, ' That men of little genius, and great bodily
" *ſtrength, are by nature deſtined to ſerve,* and thoſe of
" *better capacity to command*; and that the natives of
" Greece, and of ſome other countries, being natu-
" rally ſuperior in genius, have *a natural right to* em-
" pire ;

under the Gospel to punish them for it, as the Israelites had to punish the *Heathens*

" pire; and that the rest of mankind, being *naturally*
" *stupid*, are destined to *labour and slavery*,' (De Republ.
" lib. 1. cap. 5, 6) This reasoning is now, alas! of
" little advantage *to Aristotle's countrymen, who have*
" *for many ages been doomed to that slavery*, which, *in*
" *his* judgment, *nature had destined them to impose on*
" *others*; and many nations whom he would have con-
" signed *to everlasting stupidity*, have shown themselves
" *equal* in genius to the most *exalted of human kind*. It
" would have been more worthy of Aristotle, to have
" inferred man's natural and universal right to liberty,
" from that natural and universal passion with which
" men desire it. He wanted, perhaps, to *devise some*
" *excuse for servitude*; a practice which, to *their eternal*
" *reproach*, both Greeks and Romans tolerated even
" in the days of their glory.

" Mr. *Hume* argues nearly in the same manner in
" regard to the superiority of white men over black. 'I
" am apt to suspect,' says he, ' the negroes, and in
" general all the other species of men, (for there are
" four or five different kinds) to be naturally inferior
" to the whites. There *never was* a civilized nation
" of any other complexion than white, *nor even any in-*
" *dividual* eminent either in action or speculation. *No*
" ingenious

Heathens that were condemned in the law! Our endeavour should be rather to

"ingenious manufactures among them, *no* arts, *no* sci-
"ences.—There are negro slaves dispersed all over
"Europe, of which *none* ever discovered any symptoms
"of ingenuity." (Hume's Essay on National Charac-
"ters.)—These assertions are strong; but I know not
"whether they have any thing else to recommend
"them. For, first, though true, they would *not prove*
"*the point in question*, except it were also proved, that
"the Africans and Americans, even though arts and
"sciences were introduced among them, would still re-
"main unsusceptible of cultivation. The *inhabitants*
"*of Great Britain and France were as savage two thou-*
"*sand years ago*, as those *of Africa and America are at*
"*this day*. To civilize a nation, is a work which it
"requires long time to accomplish. And one may as
"*well say of an infant, that he can never become a man*,
"*as of a nation now barbarous, that it never can be civi-*
"*lized*. Secondly, of the facts here asserted, *no man*
"*could have sufficient evidence, except from a personal ac-*
"*quaintance with all the negroes that now are, or ever*
"*were, on the face of the earth*. Those people write
"no histories; and all the reports of all the travellers
"that ever visited them, will not amount to any thing
"like a proof of what is here affirmed- BUT, THIRD-
"LY,

to restore the *Heathens* to their lost privileges, than to harden them in
their

" LY, WE KNOW THAT THESE ASSERTIONS ARE NOT
" TRUE. The empires of Peru and Mexico could not
" have been governed, nor the metropolis of the latter
" built after so singular a manner, in the middle of a
" lake, *without men eminent both for action and specula-*
" *tion.* Every body has heard of the magnificence,
" good government, and ingenuity, of the ancient Pe-
" ruvians. *The Africans and Americans are known to*
" *have many ingenious manufactures and arts among them,*
" *which even Europeans* would find it no easy matter
" *to imitate.* Sciences indeed they have none, because
" they have no letters; but in oratory, some of them,
" particularly the Indians *of the Five Nations,* are said
" to be greatly our superiors. It will be readily allow-
" ed, that the condition of a slave is not favourable to
" genius of any kind; and yet, *the negro slaves disper-*
" *sed over Europe,* have *often discovered symptoms of inge-*
" *nuity, notwithstanding their unhappy circumstances.*
" They *become excellent handicraftsmen, and practical*
" *musicians,* and indeed learn every thing their masters
" are at pains to teach them, perfidy and debauchery
" not excepted. That a negro slave, who can neither
" read nor write, nor speak any European language,
" who is not permitted to do any thing but what his
" master

their prejudices by tolerating amongſt us a greater degree of *deſpotiſm* and *op-*
preſſion.

" maſter commands, and who has not a ſingle friend
" on earth, but is univerſally conſidered and treated as
" if he were of a ſpecies inferior to the human ;—that
" ſuch a creature ſhould ſo diſtinſtuiſh himſelf among
" Europeans, as to be talked of through the world for
" a man of genius, is ſurely no reaſonable expectation.
" To ſuppoſe him of an inferior ſpecies, becauſe he does
" not thus diſtinguiſh himſelf, is juſt as rational, as to
" ſuppoſe any private European of an inferior ſpecies,
" becauſe he has not raiſed himſelf to the condition of
" royalty.

" Had the Europeans been deſtitute of the arts of
" writing, and working in iron, they might have re-
" mained to this day as barbarous as the natives of
" Africa and America. Nor is the invention of theſe
" arts to be aſcribed to our ſuperior capacity. The ge-
" nius of the inventor is not always to be eſtimated ac-
" cording to the importance of the invention. Gun-
" powder, and the mariner's compaſs, have produced
" wonderful revolutions in human affairs, and yet were
" accidental diſcoveries. Such, probably, were the
" firſt eſſays in writing, and working in iron. Suppoſe
" them the effects of contrivance ; they were at leaſt
" contrived by a few individuals ; and if they required
" a fu-

preffion than was *ever permitted among the Jews*, or even among the ancient Heathens!

"a superiority of understanding, or of species in the in-
"ventors, those inventors, and their descendents, are
"the only persons who can lay claim to the honour of
"that superiority.
"That every practice and sentiment is barbarous
"which is not according to the usages of modern Eu-
"rope, seems to be a fundamental maxim with many
"of our critics and philosophers. Their remarks often
"put us in mind of the fable of the man and the lion.
"If negroes and Indians were disposed to recriminate;
"if a Lucian or a Voltaire from the coast of Guinea,
"or from *the Five Nations*, were to pay us a visit;
"what a picture of European manners might he present
"to his countrymen at his return! Nor would carica-
"tura, or exaggeration, be necessary to render it hi-
"deous. *A plain historical account of some of our most*
"*fashionable duellists, gamblers, and adulterers*, (to name
"no more) would exhibit *specimens of brutish barbarity*
"*and sottish infatuation*, such as might vie with any
"that ever appeared in Kamschatka, California, or the
"land of Hottentots.
"It is easy to see with what views some modern au-
"thors throw out these hints to prove the *natural inferiori-*
"*ty* of negroes. But let every friend to *humanity pray*,
"that

Heathens! for in one of our own *anti-chriſtian* colonies, even the *murder* of a negro ſlave, when under *private* puniſhment, *is tolerated* (ſee the 329th act of Barbadoes); and by the ſame diabolical act of aſſembly a man may " of *wantonneſs,* or of *bloody minded-" neſs,* or *cruel intention*" (it is expreſsly ſaid) " *wilfully kill* a negro, or *other ſlave of his own,*" without any penalty for it than a trifling fine of £15

" *that they may be diſappointed.* Britons are famous for
" generoſity ; a virtue in which it is eaſy for them to
" excel both the Romans and the Greeks. *Let it never*
" *be ſaid, that ſlavery* is countenanced by the braveſt
" and moſt generous people on earth; by a people who
" are animated with that heroic paſſion, the love of
" liberty, beyond all nations ancient or modern ; and
" the fame of whoſe toilſome, but unwearied, perſe-
" verance, *in vindicating, at the expence of life and*
" *fortune, the ſacred rights of mankind, will ſtrike terror*
" *into the hearts of ſycophants and tyrants,* and excite
" the admiration and gratitude of all good men, to
" the lateſt poſterity." Eſſay on Truth, P. 458, 459, 460, 461, 462, 463 and 464.

£15 sterling. (See remarks on this act in my tract against slavery in England, (28) p. 66 and 67.) Many instances of West-India cruelty have fallen even within my own knowledge, and I have certain proofs of no less than three married women being violently torn away from their lawful husbands, (29) even in London, by the order of their pretended proprietors! Another remarkable instance of tyranny, which

came

(28) A representation of the injustice and dangerous tendency of tolerating slavery in England. London, 1769.

(29) Nothing can be more presumptuously contrary to the laws of God, than these unnatural outrages! "Have ye not read" (said Christ himself) " that he " which made (*them*) at the beginning, made them " male and female ? and said, for this cause shall a " man leave father and mother, and shall cleave to " his wife : and they twain shall be *one flesh*. Wherefore " they are *no more twain*, but *one flesh*. What, there-" fore, GOD HATH JOINED TOGETHER LET NO MAN " PUT ASUNDER." Matth. xix. 4, 5 and 6.

came within my own *knowledge*, was the advertizing a reward (in the Gazetteer of the 1ft June, 1772) for apprehending " *an Eaſt-India black boy about* 14 " *years of age, named Bob or Pompey:*" he was further diſtinguiſhed in the advertizement by having " *round his* " *neck a braſs collar*, with a direction " upon it to a houſe in Charlotte-ſtreet, " Bloomſbury-ſquare." Thus the *black Indian Pompey* was manifeſtly treated with as little ceremony as a *black nameſake of the dog kind* could be. I inquired after the author of this unlawful and ſhameful advertizement; and found, that he was a merchant even in the heart of the city of London, who ſhall be nameleſs; for I do not want to expoſe *individuals*, but only their *crimes*. Now if maſters are capable of ſuch monſtrous OPPRESSION, *even here in England*, where their brutality renders
them

them liable to severe penalties, how can we reasonably reject the accounts of TYRANNY *in America,* howsoever horrid and inhuman, where the abominable plantation laws will permit a capricious or passionate master, with impunity, to deprive his wretched slave even of life.

I am frequently told, nevertheless, by interested persons from the West-Indies, how well the slaves are used; and that they are much happier than *our own poor at home.* But though I am willing to believe that *some few* worthy West-Indians treat their slaves with humanity, yet it is, certainly, far from being *the general case;* and the misery of our *own poor* will not be any excuse for *the oppression of the poor* elsewhere! When any of our own countrymen *at home* are miserably *poor*, it is not always clear whether themselves, or others, are to be be blamed : all we can know for certain is, that it is the indispensable duty of *every man* to *relieve them* according to his ability; and that the neglecting an opportunity of doing so, is as great an offence before God as if we had denied assistance to *Christ himself* in the same wretched condition; for so it is expressly laid down in Scripture, (30) through

---

(30) " Then shall the king say unto them on his right
" hand,—Come, ye blessed of my Father, inherit the
" kingdom prepared for you from the foundation of the
" world; For I was an hungred, and ye gave me meat:
" I was thirsty, and ye gave me drink: I was a *stranger*,
" and ye took me in: naked, and ye clothed me: I was
" sick, and ye visited me: I was in prison, and ye came
" unto me. Then shall the righteous answer him, saying,
" Lord, when saw we thee an hungred, and fed (*thee*)?
" or thirsty, and gave (*thee*) drink? When saw we thee
" a *stranger*, and took (*thee*) in, or naked, and clothed
" (*thee*)? Or when saw we thee sick, or in prison, and
" came unto thee? And the king shall answer, and
" say unto them, Verily I say unto you, inasmuch as ye
" have done (*it*) unto one of the least of these my bre-
                                    " thren,

through the mercy of God towards *the poor:* but it is obvious to whom the misery of *a slave* is to be attributed: for *the guilty possessor* will certainly be answerable to God for it; and every man, who endeavours to palliate and screen such *oppression,* is undoubtedly *a partaker of the guilt.* The *slaveholder* deceives himself if he thinks he can really *be a* CHRISTIAN, *and yet hold*

"thren, ye have done (*it*) unto me! Then shall he say
"also unto them on the left hand, Depart from me, *ye*
"*cursed into everlasting fire,* prepared for the devil and
"his angels: For I was an hungred, and ye gave me no
"meat; I was thirsty, and ye gave me no drink: I was
"a *stranger,* and ye took me not in: naked, and ye
"clothed me not: sick, and in prison, and ye visited
"me not. Then shall they also answer him, saying,
"Lord, when saw we thee an hungred, or a thirst, or a
"*stranger,* or naked, or sick, or in prison, and did not
"minister unto thee? Then shall he answer them, say-
"ing, Verily I say unto you, *inasmuch as ye did* (*it*) *not*
"*to one of the least of these, ye did* (*it*) *not to me.* And
"these shall go away into *everlasting punishment:* but the
"righteous into *life eternal.*" Matth. xxv. 34—46.

hold such property. Can he be said *to love his neighbour as himself?* (31) Does he behave to others as he would they should to him? "Ye have heard "that it hath been said, *Thou shalt* "*love thy neighbour,* and hate thine "enemy; *but I say unto you* (said our "Lord himself) *love your enemies,* &c. "That ye may be the children of your "Father which is in Heaven: for he "maketh his sun to rise *on the evil,* and "on the good, and sendeth rain *on the* "*just and on the unjust;*" (Matth. v. 44, 45) so that *Heathens* are by no means excluded from the benevolence *of Christians.*

Thus Christ has enlarged the antient Jewish doctrine of *loving our neighbours*

as

---

(31) I have examined this point more at large in a tract on "*The Law of Liberty,*" which is intended also for publication.

as ourselves; and has also taught us, by the parable of the good Samaritan, that *all mankind,* even our *professed enemies* (such as were the Samaritans to the Jews) must necessarily be esteemed our *neighbours* whenever they stand in need of our charitable assistance; so that the *same benevolence* which was due from the *Jew to his brethren of the house of Israel* is indispensably due, *under the Gospel,* to OUR BRETHREN OF THE UNIVERSE, howsoever opposite in religious or political opinions; for this is the apparent intention of the parable.

No nation therefore whatever, can now be lawfully excluded as *strangers,* according to that uncharitable sense of the word *stranger,* in which the Jews were apt to distinguish all other nations from themselves; and, since *all men are now to be esteemed " brethren and neighbours"*

"*neighbours*" under the Gospel, none of the Levitical laws relating to the bondage of *strangers* are in the least applicable to justify slavery *among Christians*; though the same laws bind *Christians* as well as *Jews* with respect to all the lessons of *benevolence* to *strangers*, which are every where interspersed therein; because these are *moral doctrines* which never change, for they perfectly correspond with "*the everlasting Gospel.*" (Rev. xiv. 6.) As for instance, "Thou shalt *not* "*oppress a Stranger,* for ye know the heart " of a *Stranger,* seeing ye were *strangers* " in the land of Egypt." Exod. xxiii. 9. This is an appeal to the *feelings* and experience of the Jews who had themselves endured a *heavy bondage,* so that it clearly corresponds with the "*royal law*" or "*law of liberty*" in the Gospel.

G   "*Thou*

"*Thou shalt love thy neighbour as thyself.*" Gal. v. 14. or as our Lord himself has more fully expressed it. "*All things whatsoever ye would that men should do to you, do ye even so to them: for* THIS IS THE LAW AND THE PROPHETS." Matth. vii. 12.

Again, "If a *stranger* sojourn with thee in your land, ye shall not vex or (oppress him) (*but*) the *stranger* that dwelleth with you, shall be unto you as one born among you, and thou SHALT LOVE HIM" (viz. *the stranger*)" AS THYSELF; for *ye were* STRANGERS in the land of Egypt. *I am the Lord your God.*" (Levit. xix. 33.) Let every slaveholder consider the importance of this command and the unchangeable dignity of him who gave it. "I AM THE LORD YOUR GOD"!--for the

"the LORD YOUR GOD is *God* of *Gods,*
"and *Lord* of *Lords,* a *great* God, a *migh-*
"*ty,* and a *terrible,* which regardeth not
"perſons" (not the Maſters more than
any ſlaves) "nor taketh reward. He doth
"execute the judgment of the fatherleſs
"and widow, and LOVETH THE STRAN-
"GER, in giving him food and raiment.
"LOVE YE *therefore the ſtranger*: for ye
"were *ſtrangers* in the land of Egypt."
Deut. x. 17, 18, 19. And how can a
man be ſaid to *love* the *ſtranger,* and
much leſs to *love him as himſelf* (ſee the
expreſs command above) who preſumes
to vex and oppreſs him with a perpetual involuntary bondage? Is this
obedience to that great rule of the Goſpel, which Chriſt has given us as the
ſum of the law and the prophets? Would
the American ſlaveholders reliſh that contemptuous and cruel uſage with which
they oppreſs their poor negroes; and

that

that the *African* (31) *strangers* should do even so to themselves without the least personal provocation or fault on their part, viz.

(31) The present deplorable state of the *African strangers in general*, ought to warn us of similar judgments against the inhabitants of these kingdoms! My own Grandfather *near a century ago* (wanting only three years, viz in 1679) warned our great national counsel of God's vengeance *by this very example*,

" *That* AFRICA (says he) which is not now more
" fruitful of monsters, than it was once of excellent-
" ly wise and learned men; that AFRICA which for-
" merly afforded us our Clemens, our Origen, our Ter-
" tullian, our Cyprian, our Augustine, and many other
" extraordinary lights in the church of God; that FA-
" MOUS AFRICA, *in whose soil Christianity did thrive*
" *so prodigiously, and could boast of so many flourishing*
" *churches, alas is now a wilderness. The wild boars*
" *have broken into the vineyard and eaten it up, and it*
" *brings forth nothing but briars and thorns*: to use the
" words of the prophet. And *who knows but* GOD *may*
" *suddenly make* THIS CHURCH AND NATION, THIS OUR
" ENGLAND, which, Jeshurun like, is *waxed fat and*
" *grown proud*, and *has kicked against God*, SUCH
" ANOTHER EXAMPLE OF THE VENGEANCE OF THIS
" KIND?"—See arch bp. Sharp's Sermons second vol. 1st Serm. which was preached before the house of Commons, April 11. 1679. (Page 22)

viz. to be branded with a hot iron, in order to be known and ranked as the cattle and private property of their oppreſſors? Like the cattle alſo to be ignominouſly compelled by the whip of a driver to labour hard " *without wages*" or recompence? If the African merchants and American ſlaveholders can demonſtrate that they would not think themſelves injured by ſuch treatment from others, they may perhaps be free from the horrid guilt of *unchriſtian oppreſſion* and *uncharitableneſs*, which muſt otherwiſe inevitably be imputed to them, becauſe their actions will not bear the teſt of that excellent rule of the Goſpel abovementioned, which Chriſt has laid down as the meaſure of our actions—" *All things whatſoever*
" *ye would that men ſhould do to you, do ye*
" *even ſo to them, for this is the law and the*
" *prophets.*" .Math vii. 12. I muſt therefore

fore once more repeat, what I have before advanced, that the permiſſion formerly granted to the Jews of holding *heathens and ſtrangers* in ſlavery is virtually repealed, or rather ſuperſeded by the Goſpel, notwithſtanding the contrary aſſertion of the African merchant, that Chriſt " *did not repeal that of ſlaves*"

The *African merchant* has alſo republiſhed the letters of his fellow advocate *Mercator*, who profeſſes in the ſame manner to draw his authority "*from Sacred hiſtory*"--" To the ſedate, " to the reaſonable, to the Chriſtian read- " ers (ſays he) I ſhall more fully ſet forth " the *lawfulneſs of the ſlave trade* from the " expreſs allowance of it in Holy writ :" (ibid appendix : B. iv.) but the very firſt inſinuation concerning the origin of ſlavery which follows this ſpecious addreſs to the ſedate &c. is founded on two *falſe aſſertions*

even

even in ONE sentence, and therefore I cannot esteem him worthy of any further notice than that of pointing out these proofs of his little regard to truth; "As "to its origin (says he) it may possibly be "derived from that sentence expressed "against Canaan *(from whom the Africans,* "says he, *are descended)* by his father No- "ah at the hour of his death. (32) Cursed "be Canaan, a servant of servants shall he be "to his brethren." But though the author afterwards allows that "both the origin "of slavery and the colour of the Africans "are incapable of *positive proof,*" yet the futility of his insinuation concerning the

descent

(32) It was not " *at the hour of his death,*" but " *when he awoke from his wine*" after he had tasted too freely the fruits of the vineyard, which he planted when he began to be a husbandman; the time therefore was probably very soon after the flood, and not *at the hour of his death,* as misrepresented by Mercator, for he lived after the flood 350 years, Genesis ix. 28.

defcent of the Africans is not like the other two circumftances " incapable of " pofitive proof." For the *Africans* are not *defcended from Canaan,* if we except the Carthaginians (a colony from the fea coaft of *the land of Canaan* who were a free people, and at one time rivalled, even the Roman common wealth, in power. The *Africans* are principally defcended from the three other fons of *Ham,* viz. *Cufh, Mifraim,* and *Phut ;* and to prove this more at large I have fubjoined to this tract a letter which I received (in anfwer to mine on the fame fubject) from a learned gentleman who has moft carefully ftudied the antiquities of the line of *Ham* : the infinuation therefore concerning the "*fentence expreffed* " *againft Canaan*" can by no means juftify the *African flave trade,* fo that *Mercator* feems indeed to write like a *mere trader,* for the fake of his iniquitous *Traffic,*
more

more than for the sake of *truth*, notwithstanding his professions of regard for the Holy Scriptures.

If we carefully examine the Scriptures we shall find, that slavery and oppression were ever abominable in the sight of God; for though the Jews were permitted by the law of Moses (on account of the *hardness of their hearts*) to keep slaves, as I have remarked in my answer to the *Reverend Mr. Thompson* on this subject (which is subjoined,) yet there was no inherent right of service to be implied from this permission, because whenever the slave could escape he was esteemed *free* ; and it was *absolutely unlawful* for any man who believed the word of God) *to deliver him up again to his master* (see Deut. xxiii. 15, 16.) whereas in our colonies, (which in acts of OPPRESSION

H may

may too juftly be efteemed *antichriftian*) the flave who *runs away* is " *deemed* " *rebellious,*" and a reward of £ 50 is offered to thofe who SHALL KILL *or* " *bring in alive any rebellious flave*" (fee the 66th act of the laws of Jamaica.) By an act of Virginia (4 Ann, ch. 49 § 37 P. 227.) after proclamation is iffued againft flaves that " *run away and lie* " *out*" it is " LAWFUL for *any perfon* " *whatfoever to* KILL a*nd* DESTROY " SUCH SLAVES *by fuch ways and means* " *as he, fhe, or they* SHALL THINK " FIT, *without accufation or impeach-* " *ment of any crime for the fame,*" &c. See the remarks on thefe, and fuch other *diabolical acts* of plantation affemblies in pages 63 to 73, of my reprefentation of the injuftice and dangerous tendency of tolerating flavery in England. Printed in 1769.

By another act of Virginia, (12 Geo.

Geo. I. chap. 4, § 8. P 368.) if a poor fellow is taken up as *a runaway* and committed to prifon, the goaler may let him out to hire, in order to pay the fees, even though he is not claimed, " *and his mafter or owner* (fays the act) " *cannot be known* ;" and in a following claufe the goaler is ordered to " *caufe a* " *ftrong* IRON COLLAR TO BE PUT ON " THE NECK *of fuch negroe or runaway,* " *with the letters* (P. G.) *ftamped thereon* ;" a moft abominable affront to human nature! our fpiritual enemy muft have had a notorious influence with the plantation law makers to procure an act fo contradictory to the laws of God, (33) and

(33) Even white fervants, *Englifh, Scotch, and Irifh* are frequently taken up by the *fheriff* and *goalers* without any warrant, or previous judgment whatever, merely " on *fufpicion of being fervants* ;" and they are then *advertized* to be *delivered up* to their tyrannical

and in particular to that (laſt cited) from Deutrenomy, viz. "Thou ſhalt
"not

rannical maſters; but though there is great injuſtice and oppreſſion in taking up theſe poor people merely "on ſuſpicion *of being ſervants*," yet it does not appear to be ſo flagrant a breach of God's command beforementioned, as the delivering up the poor runaway *negroes*, who are foreigners, and ſtrangers, and conſequently leſs capable of obtaining redreſs when they are really injured: the white ſervants are generally underſtood to be bound to their maſters only for a ſhort limited time, either with their own conſent by private contract, or as felons who are baniſhed their mother country after a fair trial *by jury* (which excludes any ſuſpicion of injuſtice) and are ſold for a certain term to pay the expences of their paſſage, &c. whereby the right of ſervice claimed from them by the maſter is more in the nature of a *pecuniary debt* than of abſolute ſlavery, ſo that the white runaway ſervant may perhaps, *as a debtor*, be delivered up to his maſter without any direct breach of the law of God beforementioned; provided there is no apprehenſion or probability of his being treated with cruelty on his return; or that the maſter would be liable to exact more ſervice than is due; in which caſe the law ought to afford protection and redreſs; but no pretences of this kind can juſtify the *delivering up* a a negroe *ſtranger!* The poor negroes are claimed *for life,*

" not deliver unto his master the ser-
" vant which is escaped from his master
" unto

life, as an *absolute property*, though (to compare their case with white servants) they never offended any member of our community either at home or abroad to justify such a severe punishment under *British Government*; neither are they capable of entering into such a *legal contract* for service, as might justify a master's claim to it, being absolutely incapacitated by *unlawful duress*, to *enter into any contract* as long as they are detained by force or fear in the *British dominions* (for which *injustice* to *strangers* the *British dominions* must sooner or later receive a severe *retribution*) and therefore *the delivering up to his master a negroe servant* "THAT HAS ESCAPED FROM HIS MASTER," and has since regained his natural liberty, must necessarily be esteemed a shameful and notorious breach of God's law. *Nevertheless our publick prints inform us even of an English man of war* and another vessel being lately sent from Grenada to the Spanish main, " to claim some " slaves that had made their escape from the Islands," (see Gazetteer June 30, 1773) the writer of the paragraph also expresses great disappointment on account of the issue of this unwarrantable and disgraceful embassy : " *instead of meeting with that justice and* " *civility which* (says he) *they had a right to expect, the* " *Governors at both places, we are told, treated them with*
" *the*

" unto thee; He shall dwell with thee,
" among you, in that place which he
" shall choose" (that is manifestly as a
free man) " in one of thy gates *where*
" *it liketh him best; thou shalt not* oppress
" him". Deut. xxiii. 15, 16. This is
clearly a *moral law,* which must be ever
binding as the will of *God;* because the
benevolent *intention* of it is *apparent,*
and must ever remain the same : for
which

" *the greatest haughtiness and contempt and refused to give*
" *them the smallest satisfaction :*" but alas the *very expectation* of better treatment (upon an errand so unlawful in itself, and so disgraceful to his Majesty's naval service) is a proof of the most deplorable degeneracy and ignorance! Even the cruel Spaniards are more civilized and shew more mercy to their slaves at present than the English, of which their new regulations for the abolishing of slavery afford ample proof, though the RETRIBUTION for their former Tyranny has lately fallen heavily on them according to the last accounts from *Chiloe* and *Chili,* which ought to be considered as merciful warnings to the rest of the world against tyranny and slavery !

which reaſon I conclude that AN AC-
TION of TROVER *cannot lye for a ſlave*;
and that no man can lawfully be proſe-
cuted for protecting a negroe, or any
other ſlave whatever, that has " *eſcaped*
" *from his maſter*" becauſe that would
be puniſhing a man for doing *his in-
diſpenſable duty* according *to the laws of
God:* and if any law, cuſtom or prece-
dent ſhould be alledged to the contrary
it muſt neceſſarily be rejected as *null and
void*; becauſe it is a maxim of the common law of England, that " *the inferior*
" *law muſt give place to the ſuperior,*
" *man's laws to God's laws*". (attorney
general Noy's maxims P. 19) And the
learned author of the *Doctor* and *Stu-
dent* aſſerts, that even *Statute law* ought
to be accounted *null and void*, if *it is ſet
forth contrary to the laws of God.*
" ETIAM SI ALIQUOD STATUTUM
" ESSE EDITUM, CONTRA EOS NUL-
" LIUS

" LIUS VIGORIS *in legibus Angliæ cense-*
" *ri debet, &c*"--- chap. vi.

The degree of servitude, which the Israelites were permitted to exact of *their brethren*, was mild and equitable, when compared with the servitude which (to our confusion be it said) is common among Christians? I have already quoted from Leviticus a specimen of the limitation to the servitude of BRETHREN; but the Jews were not only restrained *from oppressing their* BRETHREN, but were also bound by the law *to assist them generously and bountifully* according to every man's ability, when they dismissed them from their service; which is a duty too seldom practiced among Christians! (see Deutrenomy xv. 12.) " *If thy brother an*
" *Hebrew man, or an Hebrew woman, be*
" *sold unto thee, and serve thee six years;*
" *then*

" then in the SEVENTH YEAR thou shalt let him GO FREE from thee. (34) And when thou sendeft him out FREE from thee, thou shalt NOT LET HIM GO AWAY EMPTY: Thou shalt furnish him LIBERALLY out of thy flock, and out of thy floor, and out of thy wine prefs: (of that) wherewith the Lord thy God hath bleffed thee, thou shalt give unto him. And thou shalt remember that THOU WAST A BONDMAN in the land of E- gypt, AND THE LORD THY GOD RE- DEEMED THEE: THEREFORE I com- mand thee this thing to day." Thefe are the very utmoft limits of fervitude that we might venture to exact of our brethren even if we were Jews! and how much more are we bound to obferve every thing that is merciful in the law whilft we profefs Chriftianity? What then muft we think of ourfelves if we compare thefe Jewifh

limitations

(34) See alfo Exodus xxi. 2.

limitations with our Plantation laws! *A bountiful recompence* for the fervice is *plainly enjoined*, whereas the whole fubftance perhaps, of the moſt wealthy *Engliſh* or *Scotch* flaveholders would not fuffice to pay *what is due, in ſtrict juſtice*, to thofe who have *laboured in his ſervice*, if the reward is to be proportioned to their fufferings : but it ſhall one day be required of them --" *Your gold and ſilver*
" *is cankered; and the ruſt of them ſhall be*
" *a witneſs againſt you, and ſhall* EAT
" YOUR FLESH AS IT WERE FIRE : *Ye*
" *have heaped treaſure together for the*
" *laſt days.* BEHOLD THE HIRE OF
" THE LABOURERS *which have rea-*
" *ped down your fields, which is of you*
" *kept back by fraud,* CRIETH : *and* THE
" CRIES *of them* WHICH HAVE REAPED
" *are eutered into the ears of the Lord*
" *of Sabaoth*" (*or of* ARMIES) James. v. 3 and 4.

The

The *flaveholder* perhaps will say, that this text is not applicable to him, since he cannot be said to have "*kept back by* "*fraud*" *the hire of his labourers,* because he never made any agreement with them for *wages,* having bought their *bodies* of the *flave dealer,* and thereby made them his *own private property;* so that he has *a right* (he will say) *to all their labour without wages.* But this is a vain excuse for his *oppreffion,* because it is not so much *the previous agreement* as the LABOUR which renders *wages due*: for " THE LABOURER *is worthy of* HIS " HIRE" (Luke x. 7.) and the sin which " CRIETH *in the ears of the Lord of Sa-* " *baoth*" is the *ufing* a poor man's LABOUR " WITHOUT WAGES;" so that whether there is an *agreement for wages,* or *no agreement,* yet, if THE LABOUR *is performed,* the *wages are due*; and those, who keep them back, may be said to *build their houfe in unrighteoufnefs:* as the prophet Jeremiah

Jeremiah has declared in the ſtrongeſt terms (Jer. xxii. 13.) *" Wo unto him
" that buildeth his houſe by unrighteouſ-
" neſs, and his chambers by wrong; (that)
" USETH HIS NEIGHBOUR'S SERVICE
" WITHOUT WAGES, AND GIVETH
" HIM NOT FOR HIS WORK."*

And the holy Job, even before the law, declared his deteſtation of UNREWARDED SERVICE. *" If my land* (ſaid he)
*" cry againſt me, or that the furrows like-
" wiſe thereof complain:* IF I HAVE EATEN THE FRUITS THEREOF WITHOUT
" MONEY, *or have cauſed the owners there-
" of to loſe there life:* (35) *let thiſtles
" grow*

---

(35) Which was too much the caſe in the late Engliſh acquiſition of " *the fine cream part of the Iſland*" of St. Vincent's.—See authentic papers relative to the expedition againſt the Charibbs. Page 24.

"*grow instead of wheat, and cockle in-*
"*stead of barley!* Job. xxxi. 38.---40

The wife son of Sirach has also added his testimony to the same doctrine "*He that defraudeth the* LABOURER *of* "*his hire is a bloodsheder.* Ecclesiasticus xxxiv. 22. The slaveholder will perhaps endeavour to evade these texts also, by alledging, that though, indeed, he "*useth his neighbour's service* WITHOUT "WAGES, yet he cannot be said to "*give him nothing for his work,*" because he is at the expence of providing him with food and cloathing (36) and therefore this severe text is not applicable to him. But let such a one remember (if he calls himself a *Christian*) that *Christian* masters are absolutely bound to have some regard to *the interest* of their servants, as well as to their own *interest*.

"*Masters*

(36) Osnabrug trowsers, and sometimes also a Cap

"*Masters, give unto your* SERVANTS *that which is* JUST AND EQUAL, *knowing that* YE ALSO *have a* MASTER *in heaven.*" Collofs. iv. 1.

But *slaveholders* in general, have no idea of what is "JUST AND EQUAL" to be given *to servants* according to the Scriptures!

It is not a mere support in food and necessaries, as a master feeds his horse or his ass to enable the creature to perform his labour: but as *man* is superior to *brutes*, a further reward is "*just and equal*" to be given to the human *servant*. I have already sufficiently proved that *every man* under the Gospel is to be considered as our *neighbour* AND *brother*, and consequently, whatever was "*just and equal*" "to be given by a Jew, to his neighbour, or *Hebrew brother* under the Old Testament,

ment, the same must, necessarily, be considered as "*just and equal,*" and *absolutely due* from *Christians* to men of *all nations* without distinction, whom we are bound to treat *as brethren* under the Gospel *in whatever capacity they serve us.* Let the American *slaveholder* therefore remember, that *even according to the Jewish law,* (if he argues upon it *as a* CHRISTIAN *ought to do*) he is absolutely indebted to each of his slaves *for every days labour* BEYOND *the first six years* OF HIS SERVITUDE. " *In the* SEVENTH " *year* (said the Lord by Moses,) *thou* " *shalt let him* GO FREE *from thee. And* " *when thou sendest him out* FREE *from thee,* " *thou* SHALT NOT LET HIM GO AWAY " EMPTY. *Thou shalt furnish him* LI- " BERALLY *out of thy* FLOCK, &c. " *wherewith the Lord thy God hath bless-* " *ed thee, thou shalt give unto him*" &c.

If

If this was the indispensable duty *even of Jews!* how much more is it " JUST AND EQUAL to be observed by *Christians* ? The same command, when applied to the *American planter*, will include a proper stock of plants for cultivation, as Sugar-Canes, Tobacco, Indigo, &c. as well as cattle and stores, to enable a poor man to maintain himself and family upon a small farm, or lot of spare ground, lett, for a certain limited time, on reasonable terms; and renewable on equitable conditions; which are the only true means of reducing *the price of labour*, and *provisions*. Let not the planter *grudge* to part with his *servant* when he has *served* a reasonable time in proportion to *his price*, (agreeable for instance, to the regulations adopted by the *Spaniards* which I have already recommended to the *English* planters See Appendix 5.) for the word of God forbids any such base reluctance. " *It shall not* " SEEM
" HARD

"SEEM HARD UNTO THEE *when thou*
"*sendest* HIM AWAY FREE *from thee; for*
"*he hath been worth a double hired ser-*
"*vant* (to thee) *in serving thee six years;*
"*and the Lord thy God shall bless thee in*
"*all that thou doest.*" Deut. xv. 18

 The slaveholder perhaps will alledge that, though the Jews were bound to shew this benevolence to their *brethren of Israel,* yet the same laws do not bind the American planter, because his slaves are for the most part *heathens* or (as some of the negroes are) *Mahometans,* and therefore he is not bound to consider them as his *brethren;* being rather justified by the law, which permitted the Jews to keep *heathen slaves,* and "*the children of the strangers,*" in perpetual bondage &c. They shall be your *bondmen for ever*--see Leviticus xxv. 44, 45, and 46.--But I have already guarded against this

this objection, in the former part of this tract; and it muſt clearly appear, by the ſeveral points ſince mentioned, that as *Chriſtians*, we muſt not preſume to look upon any man whatever in the ſame light that the *Iſraelites* once did upon "*the children of the ſtrangers*," whether they be *black* or *white*, *Heathens* or *Mahometans*.

If a *Heathen*, or a *Mahometan*, happens to fall into our hands, ſhall we confirm his prejudices by *oppreſſion*, inſtead of endeavouring to inſtruct him as a *brother?* Surely the blood of ſuch a poor infidel muſt reſt on the guilty head of that *nominal* Chriſtian, who neglects the opportunity of adding to the number of *his brethren* in the Faith! And therefore, let that man, who endeavours to deprive others of their juſt privileges as *brethren*, take heed leſt he ſhould thereby unhappily occaſion his *own rejection*

in

in the end, when that dreadful doom, which the uncharitable muſt expect will certainly be pronounced!—For then " *the* KING" (the King of King's) " *ſhall anſwer, and ſay unto them,*— " *Verily I ſay unto you,*—*In as much as* " *ye have done* (it) *unto one of the leaſt* " *of theſe* MY BRETHREN," (for that glorious KING will eſteem even the meaneſt SLAVES AS HIS BRETHREN, if they believe in him,) "*ye have done* (it) " *unto* ME ! DEPART FROM ME YE " CURS D *into everlaſting Fire, pre-* " *pared for the Devil and his Angels."* " (Matt. xxv. 40, 41.) *I know you not !* " (xxv. 12.)—*I never knew you ;*—*De-* " *part from me ye that work iniquity!"* (Matt. vii. 23.)

Soli Deo Gloria et Gratia.

F I N I S

APPENDIX

(N°. 1.)

An ESSAY on
SLAVERY,

Proving from SCRIPTURE its Inconfiftency with HUMANITY and RELIGION;

By GRANVILLE SHARP.

" With an introductory PREFACE," (*by a Gentleman of the Law, in Weft Jerfey*) " containing the Sentiments of the Monthly Reviewers on a Tract, by the Rev. T. Thompfon, *in Favour* of the *Slave Trade*."

The Lord alfo will be a Refuge for the Oppreffed— a Refuge in Time of Trouble, Pfalm. ix- 9.

BURLINGTON: WEST JERSEY,
Printed, M.DCC.LXXIII.

LONDON: reprinted, 1776.

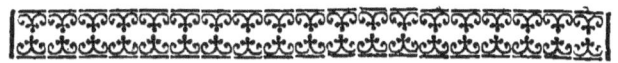

Preface by the American Editor.

'THE following Essay, though wrote,
'as the Author signifies, in haste,
'is thought to have such merit as
'to deserve a publication.—The copy was
'sent to one of the Writer's particular
'friends, whether for his own peculiar sa-
'tisfaction, or the press, is uncertain; but
'as the subject is *Liberty*, so it is expected
'the *Freedom* which is here taken, cannot
'justly give him offence, or be unaccepta-
'ble to the public.'

'IT was designed to confute a piece wrote
'by Thomas Thompson, M. A. some time
'fellow of C. C. C. entitled,' " The Afri-
" can trade for Negro Slaves shewn to be
" consistent with principles of humanity,
" and with the laws of revealed religion."
'Printed at Canterbury.'

'IN order to shew that the Essay Writer
'has not misrepresented the text, nor is
'single in his observations upon it, the sen-
'timents of the Monthly Reviewers on that
'pamphlet in May, 1772, are here insert-
'ed.'

" We must acknowledge," say they, " that
" the branch of trade here under considera-

"tion, is a species of traffic which we have
" never been able to reconcile with the dic-
" tates of humanity, and much less with
" those of religion. The principal argu-
" ment in its behalf seems to be, the *neces-*
" *sity* of such a rescource, in order to carry
" on the works in our plantations, which,
" we are told, it is otherwise impossible to
" perform. But this, though the urgency
" of the case may be very great, is not by
" any means sufficient to justify the prac-
" tice. There is a farther consideration
" which has a plausible appearance, and
" may be thought to carry some weight;
" it is, that the merchant only purchases
" those who were slaves before, and possi-
" bly may, rather than otherwise, render
" their situation more tolerable. But it is
" well known, that the lot of our Slaves,
" when most favourably considered, is very
" hard and miserable; besides which, such
" a trade is taking the advantage of the ig-
" norance and brutality of unenlightened na-
" tions, who are encouraged to war with
" each other for this very purpose, and, it
" is to be feared, are sometimes tempted to
" seize those of their own tribes or families
" that they may obtain the hoped for ad-
" vantage: and it is owned, with regard to
" our merchants, that, upon occasion, they
" observe the like practices, which are
                                    " thought

"thought to be allowable, becaufe they
"are done by way of reprifal for theft
"or damage committed by the natives. We
"were pleafed, however, to meet with a
"pamphlet on the other fide of the quef-
"tion; and we entered upon its perufal
"with the hopes of finding fomewhat ad-
"vanced which might afford us fatisfaction
"on this difficult point. The writer ap-
"pears to be a fenfible man, and capable
"of difcuffing the argument; but the li-
"mits to which he is confined, rendered
"his performance rather fuperficial. The
"plea he produces from the Jewifh law is
"not, in our view of the matter, at all
"conclufive. The people of Ifrael were
"under a *theocracy*, in which the Supreme
"Being was in a peculiar fenfe their King,
"and might therefore iffue forth fome or-
"ders for them, which it would not be
"warrantable for another people, who were
"in different circumftances, to obferve.
"Such, for inftance, was the command
"given concerning the extirpation of the
"Canaanites, whom, the fovereign Arbiter
"of life and death might, if he had pleafed,
"have deftroyed by plague or famine, or
"other of thofe means which we term na-
"tural caufes, and by which a wife Provi-
"dence fulfils its own purpofes. But it
"would be unreafonable to infer from the
manner

" manner in which the Ifraelites dealt with
" the people of Canaan, that any other na-
" tions have a right to purfue the fame me-
" thod. Neither can we imagine that St.
" Paul's exhortation to fervants or flaves,
" upon their converfion, to continue in the
" ftate in which chriftianity found them,
" affords any argument favourable to the
" practice here pleaded for. It is no more
" than faying, that Chriftianity did not
" particularly enter into the regulations of
" civil fociety at that time; that it taught
" perfons to be contented and diligent in
" their ftations: but certainly it did not
" forbid them, in a proper and lawful way,
" if it was in their power, to render their
" circumftances more comfortable. Upon
" the whole, we muft own, that this little
" treatife is not convincing to us, though, as
" different perfons are differently affected
" by the fame confiderations, it may prove
" more fatisfactory to others."

' IN another place they obferve,' " fince
" we are *all brethren*, and God has given to
" *all* men a natural right to *Liberty*, we al-
" low of no *Slavery* among us, unlefs a per-
" fon forfeits his freedom by his crimes."

' THAT Slavery is not confiftent with the
' Englifh conftitution, nor admiffable in
' Great Britain, appears evidently by the
' late folemn determination, in the court of
' King's

APPENDIX, No. 1.

'King's Bench at Weftminfter, in the cafe
' of James Somerfet, the Negro; and why
' it fhould be revived and continued in the
' colonies, peopled by the defcendents of
' Britain, and bleffed with fentiments as
' truly noble and free as any of their fellow
' fubjects in the mother country, is not eafi-
' ly conceived, nor can the diftinction be
' well founded.'

' IF " natural rights, fuch as *life* and *Li-*
" *berty*, receive no additional ftrength from
" municipal laws, nor any *human legiflature*
" has *power* to abridge or *deftroy them*, un-
" lefs the owner commits fome act that a-
" mounts to a forfeiture;" *(a)* ' If " the
" natural *Liberty of mankind* confifts proper-
" ly in a power of acting as one thinks fit,
" without any reftraint or controul unlefs
" by the *law of nature*; being a *right inhe-*
" *rent in us by birth*, and one of the *Gifts of*
" *God to man* at his creation, when he en-
" dued him with the faculty of *free will :*"
(b) ' If an *act* of Parliament is *controulable*
' *by the laws of God and nature* ; *(c)* and *in*
' *its confequences* may be *rendered void for*
' abfurdity, or a *manifeft contradiction to*
' *common reafon :* *(d)* If " Chriftianity is a
" part of the law of England;" *(e)* and
" Chrift

(a) 1 Blackftone's Commentaries, 54. *(b)* Dit.
125. *(c)* 4 Bacon's Abridg. 639. *(d)* 1 Black.
Com. 91. *(e)* Stra. Reports, 1113.

APPENDIX, No. 1.

'Chrift exprefsly commands, "Whatfoever "ye would that men fhould do to you, do "ye even fo to them," ' at the fame time ' declaring,' " for this is the law and the "law and the prophets," (f) ' And if ' our forefathers, who emigrated from Eng-' land hither, brought with them all the ' rights, liberties, and privileges of the ' Britifh conftitution—(which hath of late ' years been often afferted and repeatedly ' contended for by Americans) why is it ' that the poor footy African meets with fo ' different a meafure of juftice in England ' and America, as to be *adjudged free* in ' the one, and in the other held in the moft ' *abject Slavery?*

' WE are exprefsly reftrained from mak-' ing laws, " repugnant to," and directed ' to fafhion them, " as nearly as may be, "agreeable to, the laws of England." ' Hence, and becaufe of its total inconfif-' tency with the principles of the conftitu-' tion, neither in England or any of the ' Colonies, is there one law directly in fa-' vour of, or enacting *Slavery*, but by a ' kind of fide-wind, admitting its exiftence, ' (though only founded on a barbarous ' cuftom, originated by foreigners) attempt ' its regulation. How far the point liti-' gated in James Somerfet's cafe, would
' bear

(a) Matt. vii. 12.

'bear a sober candid discussion before an
'impartial judicature in the Colonies, I
'cannot determine; but, for the credit of
'my country, should hope it would meet
'with a like decision, that it might appear
'and be known, that *Liberty* in America,
'is not a partial privilege, but extends to
'every individual in it.'

'I MIGHT here, in the language of the
'famous JAMES OTIS, Esq; ask, "Is it
"possible for a man to have a natural right
"to make a Slave of himself or his posteri-
"ty? What man is or ever was born free,
"if every man is not? Can a father super-
"sede the laws of nature? Is not every man
"born as free by nature as his father? (*a*)
"There can be no prescription old enough
"to supersede the law of nature, and the
"grant of God Almighty, who has given
"to every man a natural right to be free.
"(*b*) The Colonists are by the law of na-
"ture free born, as indeed all men are,
"white or black. No better reason can be
"given for the enslaving those of any co-
"lour, than such as Baron Montesquieu has
"humourously assigned, as the foundation
"of that cruel Slavery exercised over the
"poor Ethiopeans; which threatens one
"day to reduce both Europe and America
"to

(*a*) 1 American Tracts by Otis, 4.   (*b*) American Tracts by Otis, 17.

" to the ignorance and barbarity of the
" darkeſt ages. Does it follow that it is
" right to enſlave a man becauſe he is black?
" Will ſhort curled hair like wool, inſtead
" of chriſtians hair, as it is called by thoſe
" whoſe hearts are hard as the nether mill-
" ſtone, help the argument? Can any lo-
" gical inference in favour of Slavery, be
" drawn from a flat noſe|| a long or a ſhort
" face? Nothing better can be ſaid in fa-
" vour of *a trade* that is the moſt ſhocking
" violation of the laws of nature; has a
" direct tendency to diminiſh every idea of
" the ineſtimable value of Liberty, and
" makes every dealer in it a tyrant, from
" the director of an African company, to
" the petty chapman in needles and pins,
" on the unhappy coaſt." (*a*)

' To Thoſe who think Slavery founded in
' Scripture, a careful and attentive peruſal
' of the Sacred Writings would contribute
' more than any thing to eradicate the er-
' ror; they will not find even the name of
' *Slave* once mentioned therein, and applied
' to a ſervitude to be continued from parent
' to child in perpetuity, with approbation.
' —The term uſed on the occaſion in the
' ſacred text is *Servant*; and, upon a fair
' conſtruction of thoſe writings, there is no
' neceſſity, nor can the ſervice, conſiſtent
' with

(*a*) American Tracts, 43, 44.

'with the whole tenor of the Scripture, be
'extended further than the generation spo-
'ken of; it was never intended to include
'the posterity.

'THF mistaken proverb which prevailed
'in that early age, "The fathers had ea-
"ten sour grapes, and the childrens teeth
"were set on edge," was rectified by the
prophets Jeremiah and Ezekiel, who declared to the people, that "they should not
"have occasion to use that proverb any
"more;—Behold all souls are mine, as the
"soul of the father, so the soul of the son,
"the soul that sinneth it shall die;—the son
"shall not bear the iniquity of the father,
"neither shall the father bear the iniquity
"of the son;—the righteousness of the
"righteous shall be upon him, and the
"wickedness of the wicked shall be upon
"him. (*a*) 'And the apostle Peter assures
'us, after the ascension of our Saviour, that
"God is no respecter of persons, but in
"every *nation* he that feareth him is ac-
"cepted of him." (*b*) 'It is also remark-
'able, that at that time, an *Ethiopian*, "a
"man of great authority," (*c*) was ad-
'mitted to the freedom of a Christian,
'whatever we may think of the colour now,
'as being unworthy of it.

'But

(*a*) Jer. xxxi. 29. Ezek. xviii. 3, 4, and 20.
(*b*) Acts x. 34. (*c*) Ditto, viii. 27.

'But admitting Slavery to be eſtabliſhed
by Scripture, the command of the Sove-
reign Ruler of the univerſe, whoſe eye
takes in all things, and who, for good
reaſons, beyond our comprehenſion, might
juſtly create a perpetual Slavery to effect
his own purpoſes, againſt the enemies of
his choſen people in that day, cannot be
pleaded now againſt any people on earth;
it is not even pretended to in juſtification
of Negro Slavery, nor can the ſons of
Ethiopia, with any degree of clearneſs, be
proved to have deſcended from any of
thoſe nations who ſo came under the Divine diſpleaſure as to be brought into ſervitude; if they are, and thoſe denuncia-
tions given in the Old Teſtament were
perpetual, and continue in force, muſt we
not look upon it meritorious to execute
them fully upon all the offspring of that
unhappy people upon whom they fell,
without giving quarter to any?'

'Many who admit the indefenſibility
of Slavery, conſidering the ſubject rather
too ſuperficially, declare it would be im-
politic to emancipate thoſe we are poſſeſſed
of; and ſay, they generally behave ill
when ſet at liberty. I believe very few
of the advocates for freedom think that
all ought to be manumitted, nay, think
it would be unjuſt to turn out thoſe who
'have

'have spent their prime of life, and now
'require a support; but many are in a
'fit capacity to do for themselves and the
'public; as to these let every master or
'mistress do their duty, and leave conse-
'quences to the Disposer of events, who,
'I believe, will always bless our actions in
'proportion to the purity of their spring.
'But many instances might be given of
'Negroes and Mulatoes, once in Slavery,
'who, after they have obtained their li-
'berty, (and sometimes even in a state of
'bondage) have given striking proofs of
'their integrity, ingenuity, industry, ten-
'derness and nobility of mind; of which,
'if the limits of this little Piece permit-
'ed, I could mention many examples; and
'why instances of this kind are not more fre-
'quent, we may very naturally impute to
'the smallness of the number tried with
'freedom, and the servility and meanness of
'their education whilst in Slavery. Let us
'never forget, that an equal if not a grea-
'ter proportion of our own colour behave
'worse with all the advantages of birth,
'education and circumstances; and we
'shall blush to oppose an equitable emanci-
'pation, by this or the like arguments.

"Liberty, the most manly and exalt-
"ing of the gifts of Heaven, consists in a
"free and generous exercise of all the hu-
"man

" man faculties as far as they are compati-
" ble with the good of society to which we
" belong ; and the moft delicious part of
" the enjoyment of the ineftimable bleffing
" lies in a confcioufnefs that we are *free*.
" This happy perfuafion, when it meets
" with a noble nature, raifes the foul, and
" rectifies the heart ; it gives dignity to the
" countenance and animates every word and
" gefture ; it elevates the mind above the
" little arts of deceit, makes it benevolent,
" open, ingenuous and juft, and adds a new
" relifh to every better fentiment of huma-
" nity." *(a)* On the contrary, " Man is
" bereaved of half his virtues that day when
" he is caft into bondage." *(b)*

'The end of the chriftian difpenfation,
' with which we are at prefent favoured, ap-
' pears in our Saviours words,' " The fpi-
" rit of the Lord is upon me, becaufe he
" hath anointed me to preach the gofpel to
" the poor ; he hath fent me to heal the *bro-*
" *ken hearted*; to preach deliverance to the
" captives ; and recovery of *fight to the blind*;
" to fet at *liberty them that are bruifed* ; to
" preach the *acceptable year of the Lord*." *(c)*

'The Editor is united in opinion with the
' author of the Effay, that flavery is contra-
' ry to the laws of reafon, and the principles
' of

(a) Blackwell's Court of Auguftus. *(b)* Homer.
(c) Luke iv. 18.

'of revealed religion; and believes it alike
'inimical and impolitick in every state and
'country; for as " righteousness exalteth a
"nation, so sin is a reproach to any people."
'(a) Hence whatever violates the purity of
'equal justice, and the harmony of true li-
'berty, in time debases the mind, and ulti-
'mately draws down the displeasure of that
'Almighty Being, who "is of purer eyes
"than to behold evil, and cannot look on ini-
"quity." (b) 'Yet he is far from censuring
'those who are not under the same convic-
'tions, and hopes to be understood with cha-
'rity and tenderness to all. Every one does
'not see alike the same propositions, who
'may be equally friends to truth, as our
'education and opportunities of knowledge
'are various as our faces. He will candidly
'confess to any one who shall kindly point
'it out: any error which in this inquiry hath
'fell from his pen. There can be but one
'beatific point of rectitude, but many paths
'leading to it, in which persons differing in
'modes and non-essentials, may walk with
'freedom to their own opinions; we may
'much more innocently be under a mistake,
'than continue in it after a hint given,
'which occasions our adverting thereto; for
'it seems a duty to investigate the way of
'truth

(a) Prov. xiv. 34. (b) Habakuk i, 13.

'truth and juftice with our utmoft ability.

' A much more extenfive and perfect view
' of the fubject under confideration, has of
' late prevailed than formerly ; and he be-
' lieves nothing is wanting but an impartial
' difinterefted attention to make ftill greater
' advances. Thus, by a gradual progreffion,
' he hopes the name of *Slavery* will be eradi-
' cated by the general voice of mankind in
' this land of *Liberty*.

' THE mode of manumitting negroes in
' New-Jerfey is fuch as appears terrific, and
' amounts almoft to a prohibition, becaufe of
' its incumbering confequences, which few
' prudent people chufe to leave their fa-
' milies liable to. It is much eafier in fe-
' veral other colonies. In Pennfylvania a
' recognizance entered into in THIRTY
' POUNDS to indemnify the townfhip, is a
' compleat difcharge. In Mariland, where
' Negroes are fo numerous, I am informed,
' the mafter or miftrefs may at pleafure
' give Liberty to their flaves without the
' leaft obligation, and be clear of any future
' burden. Both thefe are exceptionable,
' and may be improved. Proper diftinctions
' are neceffary ; for as the freedom of all
' gratis might be unjuft, not only to the
' publick but the Slave : fo any clog upon
' the owner who gives up his right at an
' age when he cannot have received much
' or any advantage from the labour of the
                                  ' individual

APPENDIX- No. 1. 17

'individual, would be unreasonable. The
'wisdom of a legislature earnestly disposed
'to do good, will I hope be directed to sur-
'mount every little difficulty in pointing
'out a scheme more equal and perfect, by
'steering a middle course; and proper care
'being kindly taken to assist and provide for
'the usefulness of those deserving objects of
'benevolence, the approbation of Divine
'Providence will I doubt not, attend such
'laudable endeavours, and crown them with
'success.—That the legislative body of each
'province in America may give due atten-
'tion to this important engaging subject,
'and be blessed to frame and establish a
'plan worthy of the united jurisprudence,
'wisdom, and benevolence of the *Guardians*
'*of Liberty*, is the sincere wish of'

THE EDITOR.

AN

ESSAY on SLAVERY,

Proving from Scripture its inconfiftency, with Humanity and Religion,

By GRANVILLE SHARP.

A REVEREND author, Mr. Thomas Thompſon, M. A. has lately attempted to prove " that the Afri-
" can trade for Negroe Slaves is con-
" fiftent with the principles of *humanity*
" and *revealed religion.*"

FROM Leviticus xxv. 39 to 46, he draws his principle conclufion, viz. " that the
" buying and felling of Slaves *is not con-*
" *trary to the law of nature,* for (fays
" he)

"he) the *Jewish conflitutions* were "strictly therewith confistent *in all* "*points*: and these are in certain cases "the rule by which is determined by "*learned lawyers* and casuists, what is, "or is not, *contrary to nature.*" I have not leisure to follow this author methodically, but will, nevertheless, examine his ground *in a general way*, in order to prevent any ill use that may be made of it against the important question now depending before the judges. *(a)*

THE reverend Mr. Thompson's *premises are not true*, for the Jewish constitutions *were not "strictly consistent"* with the *law of nature* in all points, as he supposes, and consequently his principal *conclusion* thereupon is erroneous. Many things were formerly tolerated among the Israelites, merely through the

(a) Meaning I suppose, (says the American editor) the case of Somerset, which then depended.

the mercy and forbearance of God, in confideration of their extreme frailty and inability, at that time, to bear a more perfect fyftem of law. Other laws there are in the five books (befides the cer-monial laws now abrogated) which are merely *municipal*, being adapted to the peculiar polity of the Ifraelitifh commonwealth, on account of its fituation in the midft of the moft barbarous nations, whom the Hebrews were at all times but too much inclined to immitate.

THE univerfal *moral laws* and thofe of *natural equity* are, indeed, every where plentifully interfperfed among the *peculiar laws* abovementioned; but they may very eafily be diftinguifhed by every fincere Chriftian, who examines them with *a liberal mind*, becaufe the *benevolent purpofe* of the Divine Author

is

is *always apparent* in thofe laws which are to be *eternally binding*; for " it is " *the reafon* of the law which confti- " tutes the *life of the law*," according to an allowed maxim of our own country, "Ratio Legis eft anima Legis," (Jenk. Cent. 45.) And with refpect to thefe *moral* and *equitable* laws, I will readily agree with the Reverend Mr. Thompfon, that they are the beft rule by which " learned judges and cafuifts can deter- " mine what is, or is not, *contrary to* " *nature.*"

But I will now give a few examples of laws, which are in *themfelves contrary to nature or natural equity*, in order to fhew that Mr. Thompfon's *premifes* are totally falfe:

The Ifraelites were exprefsly *permitted by the law of Mofes* to give a bill of divorce

vorce to their wives whenever they pleafed, and to marry *other women;* and the women who were put away, were alfo exprefsly permitted, by the Mofaic law, *to marry again,* during the lives of their former hufbands.

ALL which practices were manifeftly contrary to *the law of nature* in its purity, though not perhaps to *the nature of our corrupt affections and defires;* for Chrift himfelf declared, that "*from the beginning it was not fo,*"Matt. xix 8, 9. and at the fame time our Lord informed the Jews, that " Mofes, becaufe " of *the hardnefs of their hearts,* fuffered " them to put away their wives."

NEITHER was it *according to the law of nature,* that the Jews were *permitted* in their behaviour and dealings, to make a partial diftinction between their

brethren

brethren of the houſe of Iſrael, and ſtrangers. This national partiality was not, indeed, either commanded or recommended in their law—but it was clearly *permitted* or *tolerated*, and probably, for the ſame reaſon as the laſt mentioned inſtance —" thou *ſhalt not* " *lend* upon uſury to *thy brother,*" &c.— " unto *a ſtranger* thou mayeſt *lend upon* " *uſury* &c. Deut. xxiii. 19.—Again--- " of *a foreigner* thou *mayeſt exact* ;" (that is, whatſoever *has been lent*, as appears by the preceding verſes) but that which is, " thine, *with thy brother,* " thine hand ſhall releaſe," Deut. xv. 3

Now all theſe laws were " *contrary to the law of nature*" or " *natural equity,*" (whatever Mr. Thompſon, may think) and were certainly, annulled or rather *ſuperſeded,* as it were, by the more perfect doctrines of *univerſal benevolence* taught by Chriſt himſelf, who
" came

"*came not to destroy, but to fulfill the law.*"

In the law of Moses we also read, "Thou shalt not avenge or bear grudge against *the children of thy people but thou shalt love thy neighbour as thyself,*" Leviticus xix. 18.

The Jews, accordingly, thought themselves sufficiently justified, if they confined this glorious perfection of charity, viz. *the loving others as themselves,* to the persons mentioned in the same verse, viz. "*the children of their own people;*" for they had no idea that so much love could possibly be due to any other sort of *neighbours* or *brethren.* But Christ taught them by the parable of *the good Samaritan,* that *all strangers whatever* even those who are declared enemies, (as were the Samaritans to the Jews) are to be esteemed our *neighbours*

bours or *brethren*, whenever they stand in need of our charitable assistance.

"THE Jewish institution" indeed, as Mr. Thompson remarks " permited the " use of *bondservants*," but did not permit the *bondage of brethren:* STRANGERS ONLY could be *lawfully* retained as *bondmen*——" of the heathen," (or, more agreeable to the Hebrew words, מהגוים את *of the nations*) " that " are round about you; of *them* shall ye " buy *bond* men and *bond* maids. More- " over of the children of *strangers* that " do sojourn among you, *of them shall* " *ye buy*," &c.----" *They* shall be your " *bondmen for ever.*" Levit, xxv 39 to 46

THIS was the law, I must acknowledge, with respect to *a stranger* that was *purchased* ; but with respect to *a brother*

d   or

or Hebrew of the feed of Abraham, it was far otherwife, as the fame chapter teftifies;. (39th verfe) for, " if thy *bro-*
' *ther* that dwelleth by thee be waxen
" poor, and be *fold* unto thee; thou *fhalt*
" *not compel him to ferve as a bondfervant:*
" but as an hired fervant, and as a fo-
" journer he fhall be with thee, and
" fhall ferve thee unto the year of ju-
" bilee. And *then fhall he depart from*
" *thee, both he and his children with him,*"
&c. This was the *utmoft fervitude* that a Hebrew could *lawfully* exact from any of his *brethren* of the houfe of Ifrael, unlefs the fervant entered *voluntarily* into a perpetual fervitude : and, let me add, that it is alfo, the very *utmoft fervitude* that can *lawfully* be admitted *among chriftians:* becaufe we are bound as chriftians to efteem EVERY MAN *as our brother,* and *as our neighbour,* which I have already proved; fo that this confequence
which

which I have drawn, is abfolutely *unavoidable*. The Jews indeed, who do not yet acknowlege the commands of Chrift, may perhaps ftill think themfelves *juftified* by the law of Mofes, in making partial diftinctions between *their brethren* of Ifrael, *and other men?* but it would *be inexcufable* in chriftians to do fo! and therefore I conclude, that we certainly have no right to exceed the *limits of fervitude,* which the Jews were bound to obferve, whenever their poor *brethren* were fold to them : and I apprehend that we muft not venture *even to go fo far,* becaufe the laws of *brotherly love* are infinitely enlarged, and extended by the gofpel of peace, which proclaims " *good will towards men,*" without diftinction ; and becaufe we cannot be faid to " *love our neighbours* " *as ourfelves* ;" or to *do to others as we would they fhould do unto us*"---whilft we

d 2 retain

retain them againſt their *will*, in a deſpicable ſervitude as *ſlaves*, and *private property*, or *mere chattels!*

THE glorious ſyſtem of the goſpel deſtroys all *narrow, national partiality*; and makes *us citizens of the world*, by obliging us to profeſs *univerſal benevolence*: but more eſpecially are we bound, as chriſtians, to commiſerate and aſſiſt to the utmoſt of our power all perſons in *diſtreſs*, or *captivity*; whatever " the " *worſhipful* committee of the compa-" ny of merchants trading to *Africa*," may think of it, or their advocate, the reverend Mr. Thompſon.

CHARITY, indeed, begins at home; and we ought moſt certainly to give the preference to our own countrymen, whenever we can do ſo without injuſtice; but we may " *not do evil that*
" *good*

"*good may come;*" (though our statesmen, and their political deceivers may think otherwise) we must not, for the sake of *Old England*, and its *African trade*, or for the supposed advantage, or imaginary necessities of our *American* colonies, lay aside our *christian charity*, which we owe to *all the rest of mankind:* because, *whenever we do so*, we certainly deserve to be considered in no better light than as an overgrown *society of robbers*, a *mere banditti*, who, perhaps, may *love one another*, but at the same time are at enmity with *all the rest of the world.* Is this *according to the law of nature?*------For shame Mr. Thompson!

I HAVE much more to communicate, but no more time to write :---if I had, I could draw from the scriptures

the

the moſt alarming examples of God's ſevere judgments upon the Jews, for tyrannizing over *their brethren*, and, *expreſsly*, for exceeding the *limits* of *ſervitude* juſt now mentioned. *(a)* I muſt find time however to adopt one obſervation even from the reverend Mr. Thompſon, (p. 11.) viz. " This ſubject will
" grow more ſerious upon our hands,
" when we conſider the *buying and ſell-*
" *ing Negroes*, not as a clandeſtine or
" piratical buſineſs, but as an *open pub-*
" *lic trade, encouraged* and promoted by
" acts of parliament; for ſo, if being
" *contrary to religion, i t muſt be deemed* A
" NATIONAL SIN ; (*b*) and as ſuch may
" have

(a) This I have ſince accompliſhed in a tract, intituled, " THE LAW OF RETRIBUTION, &c.

(b) If this juſt remark by Mr. *Thompſon*, be compared with the above mentioned tract on *the Law of Retribution*, (wherein the uſual courſe of *God's* judge:
ments

"have a consequence that *would be* "*always to be dreaded.*" May God give us grace to repent of this abominable "NATIONAL SIN," before it is too late! If I have vindicated the law of Moses, much easier can I vindicate the benevolent apostle Paul, from Mr. Thompson's insinuations, with respect to slavery; for he *did not* entreat *Philemon* to take back his servant *Onesimus*, " in his " former capacity," as Mr. *Thompson* has asserted, in order to render bondage " *consistent with the principles of re-* " *vealed religion,*"---but St. Paul said *expresly*, " *not now* as *a servant, but,* " above

ments against NATIONS, is fairly demonstrated by a variety of unquestionable examples in the scriptures,) it will appear that nothing but *a thorough reformation* with respect to the said " NATIONAL SIN," can afford us the least room *even to hope* that THIS NATION, may escape the tremendous effects of GOD'S TEMPORAL VENGEANCE now dreadfully hanging over us!

" *above a servant,* a *brother beloved,"(a)* &c. So that Mr. *Thompson* has notoriously wrested St. *Paul*'s words.

IN the other texts where St. *Paul* recommends submission to *Servants*, for conscience-sake, he at the same time enjoins the master to entertain such a measure of *brotherly love* towards his servants, as must be entirely subversive of the *African* trade, and *West-Indian* slavery.

(a) This single circumstance one would think a sufficient bar to the inferences drawn from this epistle, in favour of slavery, by the reverend Mr. *Thompson*, and others; and yet even the learned Archbishop *Theophylact* seemed inclined to admit the same supposed *right of the master*. In the preface to his commentary on this epistle, where he gives a short account of the use and purport of it, and of the doctrines which may be deduced from it, (he says) Τρίτον, ὅτι ἃ χρη προφάσει ευλαβείας δύλες ἀποσπᾶν των δεσποτων μη βελομένων. *Thirdly. That it is not fit, through pretence of piety, to draw away servants from masters, that are unwilling to part*

flavery. And though St. *Paul*, recommends chriſtian patience under ſervitude, yet, at the ſame time, he plainly inſinuates, that it is inconſiſtent with e   chriſtianity,

part with them." But though the apoſtle declared, indeed, to *Philemon* the maſter, (v. 14.) "*without thy mind, would I do nothing* ;" &c. yet this by no means proves *the right of the maſter*, but only that the apoſtle, in love and courteſy to *Philemon*, deſired, that " *the benefit*," which he required of him, " *ſhould not be as it were of neceſſity, but willingly*," (ver. 14.) for the apoſtle's *right* to have retained *Oneſimus*, even *without the maſter's conſent*, is ſufficiently implied in a preceding verſe, (viz. 8.) " *though I might be much bold in Chriſt, to enjoin*, (or command) " *thee that which is convenient. Yet*, (ſaid the apoſtle,) "*for* LOVE's SAKE, *I rather beſeech*." &c. And a further reaſon for his not *commanding*, is alſo declared, viz. that he depended on the willing obedience of *Philemon*. " *Having confidence* (ſaid he) *in thy obedience, I wrote unto thee, knowing that thou wilt alſo do more than I ſay*." And yet that which he really did *ſay*, or require in behalf of *Oneſimus*, was as ſtrong a recommendation

Christianity, and the dignity of Christ's kingdom, that a *christian brother* should be

mendation to *favour* and *superior kindness* as could be expressed. He required him to receive *Onesimus*, "*not now as a servant, but above a servant, as a* BROTHER *beloved,*" &c. (16 verse.) that "*if he hath wronged thee, or* OWETH OUGHT," (ἡ οφειλει, in which expression even the supposed *debt of service* may be included,) "*put that on my account,*" (said the apostle, ver. 18.) which must be a complete discharge of all the master's temporal demands on *Onesimus*; and therefore it is a strange perversion of the apostle's meaning to cite this epistle, *in favour of slavery*, when the whole tenor of it is in behalf of the *slave!* But there is still a further observation necessary to be made, which puts the matter out of dispute.

Theophylact, himself, allows that *Onesimus* (at the very time he was sent back,) was *a minister of the gospel*, or a *minister of preaching* (Τȣ κηρυγματος, ‡) which is an office

‡ αλλα παλιν αποςελει προς ὑπηρεσιαν τȣ κηρυγματος, ὁ. κỳ αυτος εργατης εςι. But that he should send him back again, to the *service* of *preaching*, of which he is *a labourer*, (or minister.) Comment on the 1st. verse, page 863. edit. London, 1636.

be a *Slave*. " Can'st thou be made
" free?" (says he to the christian servants)
" *choose it rather*, for he that is *called*
" of the Lord, *being a servant*, is the
" *freeman* of the Lord; and, in like
" manner,

office of the sacred ministry, not beneath the highest order in the church, for it was the principal employment even of the apostle himself.

And this opinion of *Theophylact*, is corroborated by a variety of circumstances. By the epistle to the *Colossians*, it appears that *Onesimus* was joined with *Tychicus*, (therein declared to be a *minister*,) ‖ in an *ecclesiastical*

‖ ' *All my state shall* TYCHICUS *declare* unto you, *(*who is*) a be-*
' *loved brother*, A FAITHFUL MINISTER AND FELLOW SERVANT
' IN THE LORD; *whom I have sent unto you for the same purpose, that*
' *he might* KNOW YOUR ESTATE, AND COMFORT YOUR HEARTS
with ONESIMUS, *a faithful and beloved brother*," *(*by which it is apparent that *Onesimus* was joined in the same services, " to KNOW THEIR ESTATES AND COMFORT THEIR HEARTS,". an office that would have very ill become him, had he been sent back to his master as a SLAVE, or as Mr. *Thompson* says ' IN HIS FORMER 'CAPACITY!*)*' " *who is one of you. They(*that is *Tychicus* and *Onesimus*, jointly*) shall make known unto you all things* **which** *(*are done*) here*." *Coloss*· iv. 7. 9.

" manner, he that is called, *being free,*
" is the *servant of Christ,*"—" *Ye are*
" *bought with a price;* BE NOT THERE-
" FORE THE SERVANTS OF MEN."
The apostle, indeed, had just before

recom-

tical commission from the apostle to the church of the *Colossians*, at the very time that he was sent back to *Philemon*; § and it would surely have ill become the apostle to send back *Onesimus*, then a *minister of the gospel*, to serve his master *Philemon, in his former capacity,* (that is as a SLAVE) which is the doctrine presumed in page 18, of the reverend Mr. *Thompson's* tract; Mr. *Thompson,* as a clergyman, ought to have considered, that this would not have been for the credit of the *gospel ministry*. But *Onesimus* was not only a *minister,* and *preacher,* but afterwards even a *bishop,* which will by no means suit with Mr. *Thompson's* doctrine. The learned bishop *Fell,* testified from the authority of *the ancients,* that this *Onesimus* was a bishop. " *Onesimus*"

says

---

§ Ludov. Capellus, remarks that these epistles, (viz. to *the Colossians* and to *Philemon*) were wrote, (and consequently sent) at the same time, and after assigning several reasons for his opinion, concludes as follows, " *Ex his itaque,* (says he) *liquere puto utramque Epistolam simul eodem tempore fuisse scriptam.*" Hist. Apost. illust. page 79. ed *Genevæ,* 1634.

recommended to his disciples to abide in the same calling, wherein they were called, and, " being servants, not to care for it :" That is, not to grieve on account of *their temporal* state ; (for if, instead of thus enjoining *submission*, he had absolutely declared *the iniquity of* SLAVERY, tho' *established* and authorized by the laws of *temporal* governments, he would have occasioned more

tumult

(says he in his commentary on Colloss. iv, 5) "*servant to Philemon, a chief man in Colosse. The antients say that he succeeded Timothy, in the* BISHOPRICK *of Ephesus.*" And the great archbishop *Usher*, makes express mention of *Onesimus* in that *bishoprick*, from the authority both of *Eusebius* and *Ignatius*, (see his little tract de Episcoporum et Metropolitanorum Origine, p. 9. ed. Lond. 1687.) So that though *Paul* mentions to *Philemon* the receiving ONESIMUS FOR EVER (*that thou shouldest receive him* FOR EVER." ver. 15) yet it would be most unreasonable to conceive that the apostle meant that he should receive him FOR EVER AS A SLAVE ! The several circumstances I have mentioned, demonstrate the contrary.

tumult than *reformation* among the multitude of SLAVES, more ſtriving for *temporal* than *ſpiritual* happineſs; yet it plainly appears, by the inſinuations, which immediately follow, that he thought it derogatory to the honour of chriſtianity, that men, *who " are " bought,"* with the ineſtimable *price of Chriſt's* blood, ſhould be eſteemed *ſervants*; that is, *the Slaves*, and private property of other men; and had chriſtianity been eſtabliſhed by *temporal* authority, in thoſe countries where *Paul* preached, as it is at preſent in theſe kingdoms, we need not doubt but that he would have *urged*, nay, compelled the maſters, *as he did Philemon*, by the moſt preſſing arguments, to treat their quondam ſlaves, " NOT " NOW AS SERVANTS, BUT ABOVE " SERVANTS----AS BRETHREN BE- " LOVED."

AN
ELEGY

On the miserable STATE of an AFRICAN SLAVE, by the celebrated and ingenious WILLIAM SHENSTONE, Esq;

—SEE the poor native quit the Lybian shores,
    Ah! not in love's delightful fetters bound!
No radiant smile his dying peace restores,
    Nor love, nor fame, nor friendship heals his wound.

Let vacant bards display their boasted woes,
    Shall I the mockery of grief display?
No, let the muse his piercing pangs disclose,
    Who bleeds and weeps his sum of life away!

On the wild beach in mournful guise he stood,
    Ere the shril boatswain gave the hated sign;
He dropt a tear unseen into the flood;
    He stole one secret moment, to repine.

Yet the muse listen'd to the plaints he made;
  Such moving plaints as nature could inspire;
To me the muse his tender plea convey'd,
  But smooth'd, and suited to the sounding lyre.

" Why am I ravish'd from my native strand?
  What savage race protects this impious gain?
Shall foreign plagues infest this teeming land,
  And more than sea-born monsters plough the main?

Here the dire locusts horrid swarms prevail;
  Here the blue asps with livid poison swell;
Here the dry dipsa wriths his sinuous mail;
  O can we not here, secure from envy, dwell?

When the grim lion urg'd his cruel chace,
  When the stern panther sought his midnight prey,
What fate reserv'd me for this christian race?
  O race more polish'd, more severe than they!

Ye prouling wolves pursue my latest cries!
  Thou hungry tyger, leave thy reeking den!
Ye sandy wastes in rapid eddies rise!
  O tear me from the whips and scorns of men!

Yet in their face superior beauty glows;
  Are smiles the mein of rapine and of wrong?
Yet from their lip the voice of mercy flows,
  And ev'n religion dwells upon their tongue.

Of blissful haunts they tell, and brighter climes,
  Where gentle minds convey'd by death repair,
But stain'd with blood, and crimson'd o'er with crimes
  Say, shall they merit what they paint so fair?

No, careless, hopeless of those fertile plains,
  Rich by our toils, and by our sorrows gay,
They ply our labours, and enhance our pains,
  And feign these distant regions to repay.

           For

For them our tuſky elephant expires;
  For them we drain the mine's embowel'd gold;
Where rove the brutal nations wild deſires?—
  Our limbs are purchas'd, and our life is ſold!

Yet ſhores there are, bleſt ſhores for us remain,
  And favour'd iſles with golden fruitage crown'd,
Where tufted flow'rets paint the verdant plain.
  Where ev'ry breeze ſhall med'cine ev'ry wound.

There the ſtern tyrant that embitters life
  Shall vainly ſuppliant, ſpread his aſking hand;
There ſhall we view the billow's raging ſtrife,
  Aid the kind breaſt, and waft his boat to land."

f APPEN-

APPENDIX,

(No. 2.)

Extract of a Letter from a Gentleman in *Maryland*, to his Friend in *London*.

'BUT whether I shall go thither or
' return home, I am yet undeter-
' mined; indeed, no where shall I stay
' long from England, for I had much ra-
' ther enjoy the bare necessaries of life
' there, than the most affluent circumstan-
' ces in this country of most wretched Sla-
' very; which alone would render the life
' of any humane man most miserable.
' There are four things under the Sun,
' which I equally abhor and abominate,
' viz. *Slavery* (under which I comprehend
' all cruelty, oppression and injustice) and
' *licentiousness*, *pride* and *impudence*, all
' which abound here in a monstrous de-
' gree.
    ' The punishments of the poor negroes
' and convicts, are beyond all conception,
' being entirely subject to the will of their
                                    ' savage

APPENDIX, No. 2.

'savage and brutal masters, they are often
'punished for not doing more than strength
'and nature will admit of, and sometimes
'because they can't on every occasion fall
'in with their wanton and capricious hu-
'mours. One common punishment, is to
'flea their backs with cow hides, or other
'instruments of barbarity, and then pour
'on hot rum, superinduced with brine
'or pickle, rub'd in with a corn husk, in
'the scorching heat of the Sun. For cer-
'tain, if your judges were sensible of the
'shocking treatment of the convicts here,
'they would hang every one of them, as
'an infinitely less punishment, and trans-
'port only those, whose crimes deserve the
'severest death. Better be hanged *seven*
'hundred times, than serve *seven* years
'here! and there is no redress, for magis-
'trates and all are equally interested and
'criminal. If I had a child, I had rather
'see him the humblest scavenger in the
'streets of *London*, than the loftiest ty-
'rant in *America*, with a thousand slaves
'at his beck.'———

APPENDIX,

(N°. 3.)

A Letter from *Granville Sharp*, to *Jacob Bryant*, Efq; concerning the Defcent of the Negroes.

SIR,

'I Have conceived a very high opinion
' of your abilities, by perufing your
' learned account of *Egypt, and the Shep-*
' *herd Kings*, &c. and as you feem to have
' ftudied, very particularly, the hiftory of
' the *Cufeans* and antient *Arabians*, you
' can (I apprehend) eafily refolve fome
' doubts, relating thereto, which occurred
' to me on reading your book.
' I HAD always fuppofed that black men
' in general were defcended from *Cufh*, be-
' caufe a diftinction in colour from the reft
' of mankind, feems to have been particu-
' larly attributed to his defcendants, *the Cu-*
' *fhim*, even to a proverb.' " Can the *Cufhi*
" (commonly rendered Ethiopian) *change his*
" *Skin*," &c. (Jeremiah, xiii. 23.) and
' therefore

'therefore I concluded that all negroes,
' as well *East Indian* as *African*, are en-
' titled to the general name of *Cushim*,
' as being, probably, descended from dif-
' ferent branches of the same stock, be-
' cause the proverb is equally applicable to
' both, with respect to their complection,
' tho' in many respects they are very dif-
' ferent. But in p. 254, of your learned
' work, where you are speaking of the *Cu-*
' *seans* in general, you say, that they are
'" to be found within the tropics, almost
'" as low as the Gold coast," &c. as if you
' apprehended, that the negroes on the
' Gold coast, and below it, *were not de-*
' *scended from Cush*.

' Now, Sir, I shall think myself greatly
' obliged, if you will be pleased to inform
' me, whether you really have any particu-
' lar reason to apprehend that the negroes
' on the coast of *Guinea* (from whence our
' plantations are most commonly supplied)
' are descended from any other stock? Or
' whether their descent can at all be traced?

' I AM far from having any particular
' esteem for the negroes, but as I think
' myself *obliged* to consider them as *Men*,
' I am certainly *obliged*, also, to use my best
' endeavours to prevent their being treated
' *as beasts*, by our unchristian countrymen,
' who deny them the privileges of *human*
' *Nature* ; and, in order to excuse their
' own

'own *brutality*, will scarcely allow that
'negroes are *human Beings*.

'The tracing their descent, therefore,
'is a point of some consequence to the
'subject, in which I am now engaged for
'their defence.' * * * *

I am,

SIR,

Your most obedient,

Old Jewry,
19*th* O*ct*r. 1772.

humble Servant,

GRANVILLE SHARP.

Jacob Bryant, Esq;

APPENDIX

(No. 4.)

Mr. *Bryant*'s Anfwer to the foregoing Letter.

Cypenham, 20th Oct. 1772.

SIR,

'I MOST fincerely wifh you fuccefs in
' your laudable purpofe: and am very,
' glad to find in thefe bafe times, that there
' is a perfon, who will ftand up in defence
' of human nature; and not fuffer it to be
' limited to a fet of features and complexion.
' There is nothing, I believe, in my wri-
' tings, that can affect any argument,
' which you may think proper to urge in
' favour of thofe, whom you would patro-
' nize. But to take away all embarraf-
' ment, and uncertainty, I will give you
' my opinion upon the fubject, which you
' have ftated to me in your letter, in
' refpect to the origin of the Nigritæ or
' Negroes. You feem to think, that all,
' who are of that very deep tint, which is
' obfervable

'observable in the natives upon the coast
'of Guinea, are the offspring of *Chus*:
'and all black men in general are of the
'same origin. To this I take the liberty
'to answer, that all the natives of *Africa*
'are more or less swart: and even among
'the negroes there are a great variety of
'tints, from a light copper colour to the
'darkest black. All the inhabitants of
'this vast continent are assuredly the sons of
'*Ham*: but not equally descended from
'*Chus*. For though his posterity was very
'dark, yet many of the collateral branches
'were of as deep a die: and *Africa* was
'peopled from *Ham*, by more families
'than one. It was possessed by some of
'them, as there is good grounds to sur-
'mise, before the *Cushites* came into *Egypt*.
'We learn from scripture, that *Ham* had
'four sons, *Chus*, *Mizraim*, *Phut* and *Ca-*
'*naan*, Gen. x. v. 6. *Canaan* occupied
'*Palestine*, and the country called by his
'his name: *Mizraim Egypt*: But *Phut*
'passed deep into *Africa*, and, I believe,
'most of the nations in that part of the
'world are descended from him: at least
'more than from any other person.
'*Josephus* says, "that *Phut* was the foun-
"der of the nations in *Libya*, * and the
"people

* See Josephus, Antq. lib. 1 c. 7.

APPENDIX, No. 4.   49

" *people were from him called,* (Φυτοι)
" *Phuti.*" By *Libya* he underſtands, as the
' *Greeks* did, *Africa* in general : for the
' particular country, called *Libya* proper,
' was peopled by the *Lubim,* or *Lehabim,*
' one of the branches from *Mizraim,* Λαϐιειμ
' ᴣξ ὁυ Λιϐυες. Chron. Paſchale, p. 29.

' The ſons of *Phut,* ſettled in *Maurita-*
' *nia,* where was a country called *Phutia,*
' and a river of the like denomination.
" Mauritaniæ Fluvius uſque ad præſens
" tempus *Phut* dicitur, omniſque circa
" eum regio *Phutenſis.* (Hieron_s. Tradit.
" Hebrææ.) —— Amnem, quem vocant
" *Fut* :" (Pliny, lib. 5. c. i.)—Some of this
' family ſettled above Egypt, near Æthi-
' opia, and were ſtiled Troglodytæ. Φουᵈ
' εξ ὁυ Τρωγλοδυται Syncellus p. 47.
' Many of them paſſed inland, and peopled
' the *Mediterranean* country. In proceſs of
' time, (after their expulſion from *Egypt,*)
' the ſons of *Chus* made ſettlements upon
' the ſea coaſt of *Africa,* and came into
' *Mauritania.* Hence we find traces of
' them alſo in the names of places, ſuch as
' *Churis, Chuſares,* upon the coaſt : and a
' river *Cuſa,* and a city *Cotta,* together
' with a promontory *Cotis* in *Mauritania,*
' all denominated from *Chus* ; who at dif-
' ferent times and by different people was
' called *Chus, Cuth, Coſh* and *Cotis.* The
' river *Cuſa* is mentioned by *Pliny,* lib. 5.
'c. 1.

'c. 1. and by *Ptolomey*. Many ages after
' thefe fettlements, there was another ir-
' ruption of the *Cuſhites* into thefe parts,
' under the name of *Saracens* *, and *Moors*;
' who over ran *Africa*, to the very extre-
' mities of mount *Atlas*. They paſſed
' over, and conquered *Spain* to the north:
' and they extended themſelves ſouthward,
' as I ſaid in my treatife, to the rivers *Sene-
' gal* and *Gambia*, and as low as the *Gold
' Coaſt*. I mentioned this, becauſe I do
' not think, that they proceeded much far-
' ther: moſt of the nations to the fouth
' being, as I imagine, of the race of *Phut*.
' The very country upon the river *Gambia*
' on one ſide, is at this day called *Phuta*, of
' of which *Bluet*, in his hiſtory of *Juba Ben
' Solomon*, gives an account.

' It is not poſſible to diſcriminate at this
' æra of time the ſeveral caſts among the
' black nations, but I ſhould think, that
' we may be pretty certain, that they were
' not all *Cuſhim*, or *Cuſeans*. The Negroes
' are woolly headed; and ſo were ſome of
' the *Æthiopes* or *Cuſhim*: but nothing can
' be inferred from this: for many of the
' latter had long hair, as we learn from *He-
' rodotus*, lib. 7. c. 70. Ἰθύτριχες. We
' find

* *Query*.—Whether the *Saracens* may not rather be ſaid to be of the line of *Shem*, as being deſcended from *Abraham*?—Though indeed, both the mother and the wife of *Iſhmael*, were *Egyptians*.

‘ find from *Marcellinus*, that the *Egyp-*
‘ *tians* were *Crispi*, and had a tendency to
‘ woolly hair: fo that this circumftance can-
‘ not always be looked upon as a family
‘ characteriftic.

‘ THIS, Sir, is my opinion concerning
‘ the people in queftion, which I fubmit to
‘ your confideration, merely as matter of
‘ opinion : for I cannot pretend to fpeak
‘ with certainty. It makes very little dif-
‘ ference in refpect to the good caufe,
‘ which your humanity prompts you to ef-
‘ poufe, whether the Nigritæ are *Phutians*,
‘ or *Cufhites*. They are certainly the fons
‘ of *Ham*: and, what is more to the pur-
‘ pofe, they are the workmanfhip of God,
‘ formed in his image with a living Soul;
‘ as well as ourfelves. Confequently they
‘ deferve better treatment, than they have
‘ generally experienced from thofe, who
‘ look upon themfelves, as more enlighten-
‘ ed, and poffeffed of a greater degree of
‘ humanity. I join with you fincerely in
‘ detefting the cruel traffic : and am, with
‘ great truth, S I R,

Your moft obedient,
and moft humble Servant,
JACOB BRYANT.

‘ *P. S.* You are pleafed to obferve, *that*
‘ *a diftinction in colour from the reft of man-*
‘ *kind*

'kind seems to have been particularly attri-
'buted to the descendants of the *Cushim*. They
'certainly were very dark: but so were all
'the sons of *Ham*. And it is difficult to
'say, who were the darkest, as it was a
'circumstance depending upon the situation
'of the people spoken of, and upon many
'occult causes. The same family in differ-
'ent parts varied from itself, as I have shewn
'from *Herodotus*. The sacred writers speak
'of the *Cushi*'s complexion particularly, be-
'cause they were most acquainted with it,
'as being very near *Shem*. There were se-
'veral regions, called *Cushan* or *Æthiopia*,
'one of which was upon the confines of
'*Judæa*, near *Amalec* and *Edom*; but still
'nearer to *Midian*. Hence the prophet
'*Habbakuh* says in a vision,—" *I saw the
"tents of* Cushan *in affliction, and the cur-
"tains of* Midian *did tremble.*" C. iii. v. 7.
'These were the *Araba Cushitæ*; with
'whom the *Israelites* were most acquainted.
'Of the sons of *Phut*, and of the *Ludim*,
'*Lehabim*, and other descendants of *Ham*,
'in *Africa*, they had probably little or no
'cognizance, excepting only the *Mizraim*,
'and the *Æthiopians* immediately above
'them to the south of *Syene*. With these
'they were acquainted. Should it be in
'my power to give you any farther satisfac-
'tion, I shall be very proud of your com-
'mands. * * * * * *

'THE whole of what you mention, that
'all Moors, Negroes, and black perfons are
'from one common ftock is moft affuredly
'true, if you make the head of that family
'*Ham*, inftead of *Chus*. One remove higher
'makes every thing ftrictly confonant to
'the truth.'

APPENDIX,

(No. 5.)

The Regulations lately adopted by the *Spaniards*, at the *Havanna*, and some other Places, for the gradual *enfranchisement of Slaves*, are to the following Effect.

' AS soon as a slave is landed, his
' name, price, &c. are registered in
' a public register; and the master is oblig-
' ed, by law, to allow him *one working day*,
' in every week, to himself, *besides Sundays*;
' so that, if the slave chuses to work for his
' master on that day, he receives the *wages*
' *of a freeman* for it; and whatever he gains
' by his labour, on that day, is so secured to
' him by law, that the master cannot de-
' prive him of it. This is certainly a con-
' siderable step towards the abolishing *abso-*
' *lute slavery*. As soon as the slave is able
' to purchase *another working day*, the mas-
' ter is obliged to sell it to him at a propor-
' tionable price, viz. one fifth part of his
' original

'original coft; and fo, likewife, the re-
'maining four days, at the fame rate, as
'foon as the flave is able to redeem them;
'after which *he is abfolutely free*: This is
'fuch encouragement to induftry, that even
'the moft indolent are tempted to exert
'themfelves. Men, who have thus work-
'ed out their freedom, are enured to the
'labour of the country, and are certainly
'the moft ufeful fubjects that a colony can
'acquire. Regulations might be formed
'upon the fame plan to encourage the in-
'duftry of flaves *that are already imported
'into the colonies*, which would teach them
'how to maintain themfelves, and be *as
'ufeful*, as well as *lefs* expenfive to the plan-
'ter. They would by fuch means become
'members of fociety, and have an intereft
'in the welfare of the community; which
'would add greatly to the ftrength and fe-
'curity of each colony : whereas, at pre-
'fent, many of the plantations are in *conti-
'nual danger of being cut off by their flaves,
'a fate which they but too juftly deferve.*'

APPENDIX,

(No. 6.)

Extract of a Letter from the Author, to a Gentleman at *Philadelphia*.

'—— and surely there needs no argu-
' ment to demonstrate the weakness and dan-
' ger of the more southern colonies, from *the*
' *immense multitude of slaves*, that are forci-
' bly detained therein !

' THE congress have acted nobly in for-
' bidding the iniquitous importation of *more*
' *slaves* ; but the business is but half done,
' 'till they have agreed upon some equitable
' and safe means of *gradually enfranchising*
' those which remain. No time should be
' lost in forwarding this equitable measure ;
' —and, to secure the affections of the ne-
' groes, assurances should be immediately
' given of such friendly intentions towards
' them, lest any attack should, in the mean
' while, be made in those quarters, which
                                        might

' might encourage *an infurrection*. I tremble
' for the probable confequences of fuch an
' event! for though *domeftic flavery*, (which
' I deteft from my heart) would thereby be
' abolifhed, yet that effect would be wrought
' at the expence of *public Liberty*; and the
' *tyranny* and injuftice of private individuals
' would feem, perhaps, to be too feverely
' punifhed by that horrid carnage and im-
' placability, which ufually attend the con-
' flicts between mafters and flaves!

' LET *private intereft* therefore give place
' to *juftice* and *right*, which will moft effec-
' tually adminifter to the public fafety.

' LET it be remembered that many of
' the negroes are natives of the colonies,
' and confequently have *a natural right* to a
' *free exiftence* therein, as well as the Land-
' holders themfelves. I fhall not prefume
' to *advife* the mode of effecting this im-
' portant and neceffary enfranchifement,
' but will only offer a few hints in order to
' promote the confideration and determina-
' tion of thofe who are beft able to judge
' of the matter.

' SUPPOSE the value of every flave now in
' the colonies, was to be fairly eftimated, by
' juries appointed for that purpofe, and the
' value to be entered, under their infpection,
' (as a pecuniary *debt* due from each negroe
' to his mafter,) in a public regifter for each
' diftrict. Suppofe alfo that the landholders,

h ' who

' who do not occupy all their grounds, were
' advised to divide what lands they can spare
' into *compact little farms*, with a small wooden
' cottage to each, which should be allotted
' to those negroes only, who are natives of
' the colony, or else have been so long in it,
' that their dispositions are sufficiently known,
' whether or not they may safely be entrust-
' ed with their liberty. Let such negroes hold
' these small portions of land by leases, for
' a certain term of years; and at equitable
' rents, to be paid in such portions of *the
' produce* from time to time, as shall be
' thought most reasonable, leaving the ten-
' ants a moderate gain, (besides their necef-
' sary subsistence) to encourage industry, and
' yet so as to yield the landlords a due profit
' from each portion of their estates, besides
' an adequate allowance to reimburse (within
' the limited time) not only the registered
' price of their quondam slaves, but also
' whatever sums they may have advanced to-
' wards the expence of *building*, of *implements*,
' of *live stock*, of *seed*, &c. &c. the amount
' of which ought to be added to the first
' debt and registered, in like manner, before
' the leases are executed. By these means the
' landlords will lose nothing of their wealth,
' and yet the most useful and worthiest of the
' negroes will acquire a *natural interest* in
' the welfare and safety of the community,
' which will insure their assistance against
                                        ' any

'any hoſtile attempt of the reſt. Other
' negroes, that are not capable of managing
' and ſhifting for themſelves, nor are fit to be
' truſted, all at once, with liberty, might be
' delivered over to the care and protection of
' a county committee, in order to avoid the
' baneful effects of *private property in men*;
' and might, by the ſaid committee, be let
' out, as *hired ſervants*, to ſuch perſons as
' would undertake the charge of them, to
' be paid (alſo *in produce*) towards the dif-
' charge of the regiſtered debt for each
' man's original price; and the labourer
' himſelf in the mean while to be allow-
' ed one day in a week (beſide the Sun-
' day) for his own profit, or be paid
' for it according to the mode of the
' *Spaniſh regulations*, (which I before tranſ-
' mitted) that he may have an opportuni-
' ty to acquire a little property of his own,
' which will *prepare his mind*, as well as
' his circumſtances *for freedom*, by enabling
' him, as a member of the community to
' ſhift for himſelf at the time of his dif-
' charge. By ſome ſuch regulations, as
' theſe, ſlavery might be changed into a
' condition, more nearly reſembling that of
' *hired ſervants*, as no maſter would be the
' *abſolute proprietor* of thoſe he employs,
' and yet all reaſonable advantages ariſing
' from their labour, would remain; which
' muſt occaſion a reciprocal improvement
' in the morality and humanity both of maſ-
' ters

'ters and servants; and in procefs of time,
'inftead of *wretched slaves*, a new and ufe-
'ful order of men, at prefent unknown in
'America, (where every *freeman* cultivates
'his own ground only) would be eftablifhed
'amongft you; I mean a hardy body of
'*free peasants*, ferving either as *trusty ten-
'ants* or *farmers*, to improve the eftates of
'landed gentlemen, or elfe as *laborious cot-
'tagers*, who might be employed with in-
'finite advantage to the neighbourhood,
'wherever eftablifhed, efpecially if they
'were encouraged by an allotment of a
'fmall patch of land for a potatoe ground
'or garden, with a right of pafture for a
'little live ftock upon fome common field
'in the neighbourhood of their little cot-
'tages.—Landholders by this means would
'have their eftates better peopled and im-
'proved, and yet avoid the guilt and dan-
'ger of oppreffion. In the mean while, the
'hours of labour fhould be uniformly regu-
'lated, to prevent the oppreffion of avari-
'cious exactors, and the danger of difcon-
'tent: and fchools fhould be opened in
'every diftrict, to give the poor labourers
'and their children, fome general ideas of
'morality and religious knowledge, which
'conftitute the moft effectual *bond of peace*.
'Thefe regulations I mention only by way
'of hint: you have the fame earneft regard
'for

'for the caufe of *general liberty*, and *the
natural rights of mankind* that I have,
and much greater abilities to defend them,
and to propofe a more perfect fyftem than
what is here fuggefted. Let me therefore
intreat you to confider this matter, and to
forward, as foon as poffible, fome fcheme
of general enfranchifement, becaufe American liberty cannot be firmly eftablifhed
'till this is done.

'I am with great efteem,

'Dear SIR,

'Your affectionate friend

'and humble fervant.'

London,
18 July, 1775.

'GRANVILLE SHARP.'

APPENDIX,

(No. 7.)

Extract from Mr. *Morgan*'s Book, intituled, ' *A Plan for the Abolition of Slavery, in the West Indies.*'

—Page 12.——' Nothing can be more
' oppofite to every idea of juftice and mo-
' rality than the prefent practice of buying
' flaves, to cultivate the Weft Indian iflands
' and the fouthern provinces on the conti-
' nent of America; nor can any thing, I
' think, be eventually more fatal — * * *

Page 13.——' Yet fomething, out of
' worldly prudence, ought to be done;—for,
' as this evil has been violently introduced,
' contrary to the natural courfe of things
' and the conftitution of the world, it will
' one day find a remedy even in its excefs.
' Matters will be fatally brought to a crifis,
' and nature will vindicate her own laws,
' and

' and restore the credit of her equal and
' just administration, to the lasting punish-
' ment of those who abused it. THIS WILL
' BE WHEN THE BLACKS OF THE SOUTH-
' THERN COLONIES ON THE CONTINENT
' OF AMERICA SHALL BE NUMEROUS
' ENOUGH TO THROW OFF AT ONCE THE
' YOKE OF TYRANNY TO REVENGE THEIR
' WRONGS IN THE BLOOD OF THEIR OP-
' PRESSORS, AND CARRY TERROR AND
' DESTRUCTION TO THE MORE NORTHERN
' SETTLEMENTS. Such a revolution can-
' not take place in the islands until this
' period, on account of the want of intel-
' ligence and communication between the
' slaves of one island and another, and of
' the easy communication and mutual af-
' sistance of whites. But an insurrection on
' the continent, once communicated, will
' be an incitement in the islands, and a sig-
' nal for a general and (but that every
' Englishman is alike concerned, and the
' planter not peculiarly criminal) A MERIT-
' ED CARNAGE.

' Nothing can be conceived MORE DE-
' STRUCTIVE, MORE INSATIATE, THAN
' THE WARS WHICH WILL FOLLOW THIS
' EVENT; they will be every where marked
' with THE MOST HORRIBLE CRUELTIES,
' and THE MOST FURIOUS REVENGE. The
' distinction of *black* and *white*, which we
' have

'have so unreasonably made the marks of
'*freedom* and *slavery*, will then become
'the obvious colours of mutual hostility and
'revenge; and it seems likely that these
'wars MAY END TO THE DISADVANTAGE
'OF THE WHITES; because the blacks, as will
'be presently observed, will increase faster,
'and because their nature seems better able
'to bear the severity of cold, than the
'whites can that of heat.'—&c.

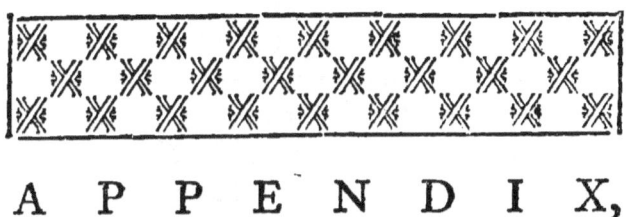

APPENDIX,

(No 8.)

A Copy of what "*is said* to be the "subſtance of Lord *Mansfield*'s ſpeech "in the caſe of *Somerſet* and *Knowles:*"

ON Monday the 22d June, in Trinity term, 1772, the court of *King's Bench*, proceeded to give judgement in the Caſe of *Somerſet* and *Knowles*, upon the return of the Habeas Corpus. LORD MANSFIELD firſt ſtated the return; and then ſpoke to the following purport, which is taken from the ſecond edition of a Tract, printed in 1773, intituled, " *Conſidera-* " *tions on the Negroe Cauſe, ſo called, ad-* " *dreſſed to the right honourable lord* Mans- " field, *lord chief juſtice of the court of* " *King's Bench, by* SAMUEL ESTWICK, " *A. M. Aſſiſtant Agent for the iſland of* " Barbadoes." page vii. viz.

'WE pay due attention to the opinion
' of Sir *Philip Yorke* and Mr. *Talbot*, in
' the year 1729, by which they pledged
' themſelves to the Britiſh planters for the

'legal

'legal confequences of bringing Negroe-flaves
'into this kingdom, or their being baptiz-
'ed; which opinion was repeated and re-
'cognized by lord Hardwicke, fitting as
'chancellor, on the 19th of October, 1749,
'to the following effect: he faid,' "that
"trover would lay for a negroe-flave: that a
"notion prevailed, that if a flave came into
"England, or became a Chriftian, he there-
"by became emancipated; but there was no
"foundation in law for fuch a notion: that
"when he and Lord Talbot were attorney
"and folicitor general, this notion of a flave
"becoming free by being baptized per-
"vailed fo ftrongly, that the planters induf-
"trioufly prevented their becoming chrif-
"tians: upon which their opinion was taken;
"*and upon their beft confideration they were*
"*both clearly of opinion,* that a flave did not
"in the leaft alter his fituation or ftate to-
"wards his mafter or *owner,* either by be-
"ing chriftened, or coming to England:
"that though the ftatute of Charles II. had
"abolifhed" *(homage ‡)* "tenure fo far,
"that no man could be a *Villein regardant;*
"yet if he would acknowledge himfelf a
"*Villein* engroffed in any court of record, he
' knew

(‡) See a part of my lord *Mansfield*'s fpeech printed
in the Appendix, (p. 11.) of "*a Treatife upon the*
"*Trade from* Great Britain *to* Africa, *by an African*
"*merchant,*" wherein this word "*homage*" is inferted.

" knew of no way by which he could be en-
" titled to his freedom, without the confent
" of his mafter." ' We feel the force of
' the inconveniences and confequences that
' will follow the decifion of this queftion :
' yet all of us are fo clearly of one opinion
' upon the *only* queftion before us, that we
' think we ought to give judgment without
' adjourning the matter to be argued before
' all the judges, as ufual in the habeas cor-
' pus, and as we at firft intimated an inten-
' tion of doing in this cafe. The only quef-
' tion then is, *Is the caufe returned fufficient*
' *for the remanding him? If not,* he muft be
' difcharged. The caufe returned is, the
' *flave* abfented himfelf and departed from
' his mafter's fervice, and refufed to return
' and ferve him during his ftay in *England*;
' whereupon, by his mafter's orders, he was
' put on board the fhip by force, and there
' detained in fecure cuftody, to be carried
' out of the kingdom and fold. So high
' an act of dominion muft derive its autho-
' rity, if any fuch it has, from the law of
' the kingdom *where* executed. A foreig-
' ner cannot be imprifoned *here* on the au-
' thority of any law exifting in his own coun-
' try. The power of a mafter over his fer-
' vant is different in all countries, more or
' lefs limited or extenfive, the exercife of
' of it therefore muft always be regulated
' by

APPENDIX, No. 8.

' by the laws of the place where exercised.
' The state of slavery is of such a nature,
' that it is incapable of being now intro-
' duced by courts of justice upon mere rea-
' soning, or inferences from any principles
' natural or political; it must take its rise
' from *positive law*; the origin of it can in
' no country or age be traced back to any
' other source. Immemorial usage preserves
' the memory of *positive law* long after all
' traces of the occasion, reason, authority,
' and time of its introduction, are lost, and
' IN A CASE SO ODIOUS AS THE CONDITION
' OF SLAVES MUST BE TAKEN STRICTLY.
' *(Tracing the subject to natural princi-*
' *ples, the claim of slavery never can be sup-*
' *ported.)* (‡) THE POWER CLAIMED BY
' THIS RETURN WAS NEVER IN USE
' HERE: (or *acknowledged by the law.*) No
' master ever was allowed here to take a
' slave by force to be sold abroad because he
' had deserted from his service, or for any
' other reason whatever; WE CANNOT SAY,
' *the cause set forth by this return* IS ALLOW-
                                            ' ED

(‡) These additions in Italics between hooks before and after the words " THE POWER CLAIMED BY THIS RETURN WAS NEVER IN USE HERE," are taken from the notes of a very ingenious and able counsellor, who was present when the judgement was given.—The rest of his notes sufficiently agree in substance with what Mr. *Estwick* has printed.

APPENDIX, No. 8.

'ED OR APPROVED OF BY THE LAWS OF
'THIS KINGDOM, and therefore the man
'must be discharged.'

Upon this Mr. *Estwick* has been pleased to observe as follows, '*I must confess* (says he) *I have been greatly puzzled in endeavouring to reconcile this judgement with this state of it, and with my comprehension,*' &c. But the writer quoted by the *African merchant* before mentioned, is not so modest in his censure of this judgement, nor so honest in his *recital* of it, as Mr *Estwick*, for he partially conceals the most material part of the learned judge's speech, because it happens to make against his own wicked cause; and tells us by way of excuse for so notorious and partial an omission—that " *the remainder of the speech is too vague to come into consideration,*' &c. (p. 12.) Another anonymous writer (author of a pamphlet, intitled 'CANDID REFLECTIONS *upon* THE JUDGEMENT *lately awarded by the Court of King's Bench, in Westminster Hall, on what is commonly called the* NEGROE CAUSE, *by a Planter,*') after comparing this JUDGEMENT of the King's Bench, with the opinions of the judges *Holt* and *Powel*, and those of the attorney and solicitor general, *York* and *Talbot*, &c. is pleased to *reflect* thereupon as follows. " *A point,* (says he) *upon which these great Oracles of the law have published*

" *such*

"*such opposite sentiments, seems as far as ever*
"*from being established upon the solid ground of*
"*absolute* PRECISION. *The planters of course*
"*have been left* (says he) *as much puzzled*
"*by this* DELPHIC AMBIGUITY, *as the sages*
"*themselves appear to have been, in forming*
"*their judgements upon the subject. The mat-*
"*ter having been* CONFOUNDED *in this*
"GRAND UNCERTAINTY," &c. (p. 57.)
But these heavy charges of the want of
" PRECISION," of " DELPHIC AMBIGUITY,"
and of being " CONFOUNDED in GRAND UN-
"CERTAINTY," &c. are so far from being
" CANDID REFLECTIONS," (as this author
would have us believe them,) that even *his
own evidence* on the preceeding page, clearly proves the falshood and injustice of his
censures; for he has there given us the
EFFECT of that late judgment of the court
of King's Bench, in THE CLEAREST TERMS,
without the least *doubt* or *difficulty*; so that
the *delphic ambiguity*, of which he *immediately after* complains, must be *(*even according to his own evidence,*)* a mere *calumny!*

After reciting the opinion of lord chief
justice *Holt*, he immediately adds as follows.

" Lord chief justice mansfield (says he)
" adds to this effect.
" That the laws of Great Britain do not
" authorize a master to reclaim his fugi-
" tive SLAVE, confine or transport him out of
" the kingdom. In other words;" (says
he)

he) " that a negroe flave, coming from the " colonies into *Great Britain* becomes, *ipfo* " *facto*, FREE."

Thus, notwithftanding the *un-candid reflections* of this author about DELPHIC AMBIGUITY, yet even *he himfelf* has without *doubt* or *difficulty*, declared THE *certain* and *unavoidable* EFFECT of the judgement delivered by Lord *Mansfield!* That this author (notwithftanding his prejudices, and unjuft cenfures about ambiguity) has really ftated the *certain* and *unavoidable* EFFECT of the faid judgment, will appear by the following remarks upon it.

APPENDIX,

(No. 9.)

Remarks on the Judgment of the Court of *King's Bench*, in the Cafe of *Stewart* and *Somerfet*. By *Granville Sharp*.

THIS judgment will not appear doubtful and inexplicit, (as fome have too haftily efteemed it) if the whole be taken together, and THE EFFECT of it be duly confidered.

LORD *Mansfield* pronounced the fentiments or judgment *of the whole bench*, and therefore if any thing was wrong, the blame ought not to reft on him alone; neverthelefs, if we fairly examine what was faid, we fhall find no room for blame or cavil. His lordfhip faid, " WE *pay due*
' *attention* to the opinion of Sir *Philip*
' *York* and Mr. *Talbot*, in the year 1729,'

Now

Now the purport of that opinion was, that the master '*may legally compel* his flave ' *to return to the plantations.*'

LORD *Mansfield* modestly declined giving a direct contradiction, in express words, to the opinion of two such very eminent and learned lawyers; but chose rather to condemn it, tacitly, by *the effect* of the judgment, which he was about to pronounce; and therefore he merely recited the opinion without the least comment, and proceeded to the determination of the court upon the case before them; which is clear and incontrovertible with respect to the main point of the question, viz. the power claimed by the master, of carrying away his flave by force.

' *The power claimed by this return,* (said the ' chief justice) *was never in use here, or ac-* ' *knowledged by the law.*' Now it was certainly the duty of the court to give judgment according to *the known laws,* and not to be influenced by *any opinion* whatsoever.

THEY acknowledged, indeed, the having " *paid due attention*" to the said opinion; but as their determination was diametrically opposite to the assertions in that opinion, it is manifest, that the court *did not think it grounded in law,* according to which alone they were bound to determine. The conclusion of lord *Mansfield's* speech contains

more

more substantial and unanswerable reasons for the judgment he was about to give, than the generality of his hearers, perhaps, were aware of; for he very ingeniously expressed in the small compass of two short sentences, that the masters claim was contrary to three principal foundations of the *English* law, viz. NATURE, USE, (or *Custom*,) and the WRITTEN LAW; which last also includes two other foundations, viz. MAXIMS and STATUTES. With respect to the first, he said — " *traceing the subject to* NATURAL *princi-*
" *ples, the claim of* SLAVERY *never can be*
" *supported.*" With respect to the second, he said, " *The power claimed by this return, was*
" *never in* USE *here,*" and thirdly, that it was
" never *acknowledged by* THE LAW."

THESE seem to have been *the reasons* of the determination; and consequently the court was obliged *by the common law* (which always favours LIBERTY) ‖ to discharge the man from the *unnatural* and *unprecedented* claims of his master, which was accordingly done, so that the true meaning of this determination is rendered clear and incontrovertible, as well by *the effect of it*, as by the unanswerable *reasons* above mentioned.

THAT

‖ ' *Law favoureth life,* LIBERTY, *and* DOWER.'
' *Law regards the* PERSON *above his possessions,*----LIFE
' *and* LIBERTY, *most,*' &c. (Principia Legis et Æquit. p. 56.
' LIBERTAS *est res inestimablis.*' (Jenk. Cent. 52.)

THAT there is nothing *doubtful* or *inexplicit* in this *judgement*, delivered by lord *Mansfield*, will further appear by the following report of a cafe in the PREROGATIVE COURT, wherein this very determination on *Somerfet*'s cafe, is exprefsly cited, and the EFFECT of it clearly and fully declared by a learned judge of that court. And the propriety of the faid judgment has very lately been ftill further confirmed by a decree alfo in THE HIGH COURT OF ADMIRALTY, after a very learned and folemn debate concerning the *legality*, or, *illegality of flavery in England*, wherein the merits of the queftion on both fides was fully examined and difcuffed. A fhort ftate of the Cafe, together with the fubftance of the decree will be found in Appendix, No. 11. The offence expreffed in this latter Cafe was fo flagrantly wicked in all its circumftances, and upon the whole, was fo notorious a contempt of the laws and conftitution of this kingdom, as well as of *natural right*, and common honefty, that all perfons, who have any regard for juftice, muft be moved with indignation againft the authors of the milchief, and muft wifh to fee them corrected by fome *adequate* and *exemplary punifhment*, inftead of a decifion againft them for the mere *recovery of wages*. In order therefore to prevent any unjuft prejudice of well meaning people, againft the manner of proceeding in this cafe for redrefs, it is neceffary

k 2

cessary to remark, that the negroe did not 'apply for redress of these injuries,' till more than two years after they were committed, whereby he was deprived of the *satisfaction* to which THE HABEAS CORPUS ACT would otherwise have entitled him 'IN ANY OF HIS MAJESTY'S COURTS OF RECORD,' viz.— '*to recover his treble costs, besides damages, which damages so to be given*, (says the act) *shall not be less than* FIVE HUNDRED POUNDS,' that is *five hundred pounds* from *each* offender,—frm *every individual* concerned (and these seem, in the present case, to have been more than 4 or 5) that had either been 'advising, aiding, or 'assisting,' in so flagrant a breach of the peace; and they would likewise have been subject to all the '*pains, penalties, forfeitures, losses* or *disabilities* ordained in THE STATUTE of PROVISION and PRÆMUNIRE! See my 'Representation of the injustice, and dangerous tendency of tolerating Slavery in *England*,' printed in 1769, pages 25 to 29.

GRANVILLE SHARP.

APPEN-

APPENDIX,

(No. 10.)

CASE,

Prerogative Court, May 11th, 1773.
CAY and CRICHTON.

——A. B. deceafed, *in* 1769, among other effects, left behind him a *negroe fervant*. CRICHTON, the executor, was called upon by CAY, to give in an *inventory* of the deceafed's *goods and chattels*, which he accordingly did, but omitted the *negroe*.

This omiffion was made a ground of exception to the inventory, as being, therefore, not *perfect*.

UPON argument, it was faid by the council on behalf of *Crichton*, that by a very late cafe in the King's Bench, of *Knowles*

and

(a) and Somerset, negroes were declared *to be free in England,* and consequently, they could not be the subjects of *property,* or be considered as any part of a personal estate.

It was answered, that the case abovementioned was determined only in 1772; that A. B. died in 1769, at which time negroes were in some respects, considered as property, and therefore that he ought to have been included in the account,

The judge (Dr. *Hay,*) said that this court had no right to try any question relating to freedom and slavery; but as *Negroes* had been *declared free* by the court which had the proper jurisdiction, that determination referred to them, as well at the preceeding time, as at the present, and therefore directed, that article, in which the *negroe* was mentioned, to be struck out of the *exceptive allegation.*

(a) *Knowles* was the master of the ship who detained *Somerset,* by order of Mr. *Stewart,* who claimed the latter as his *property.*

APPENDIX,

APPENDIX,

(No. 11.)

High Court of Admiralty, before Sir Geo. Hay, *Knt. L.L.D.* June, 29, 1776.

CASE.

ROGERS, alias *RIGGES* againſt *JONES*.

Dr. *Wynne*   Dr. *Harris*
Dr. *Bever*   Dr. *Calvert*
Proctor *Torriano.* Proctor *Holman.*

'GEORGE ROGERS alias RIGGES,
' a negro about nineteen years of age, had
' been a ſervant to ſeveral gentlemen in
' *England,* and in the ſummer of 1766,
' being

'being then out of place, became ac-
' quainted with *John Latter* and *John*
' *Seffins*, who contracted with *Arthur Jones*
' for the sale of him; an assignment
' was accordingly drawn for that purpose,
' and signed by *John Latter*, by which
' *Rogers* was transferred to Messrs. *Mason*
' and *Jones*, as a slave, for the sum of
' twelve guineas.

' SOME time in August, 1766, after the
' sale above mentioned, *Rogers*, under some
' false pretences, was carried on board the
' ship *Britannia*, then lying at *Deptford*, of
' which Messrs. *Mason* and *Jones* were owners,
' was there detained against his will, and that
' he might not escape, was carried down into
' the sail room, by order of the chief mate,
' and the gratings were put upon him. In
' this confinement he was kept, till the ship
' set sail, when he was released, and suffer-
' ed to go about upon deck; but not being
' entered in the ship's books as a mariner,
' nor having any particular office, or wages
' assigned to him, he was set to work about
' the ship's duty in general, till he was ap-
' pointed as an assistant to the cook, which
' office he executed sometimes as assistant,
' and sometimes as principal cook, during
' the whole voyage. The ship first sailed to
' the coast of *Africa*, on the SLAVE TRADE,

and

' and from thence to *Porto Rico*, where he
' was offered to fale, by the captain of
' the *Britannia*, as a prime flave; but
' *Rogers* having found an opportunity
' of relating his ftory to the *Spanifh*
' merchants, they refufed to purchafe
' him; he therefore returned with the
' fhip, in which he ftill acted in his
' former capacity of affiftant cook; and
' upon their arrival in the port of *Lon-*
' *don*, in *May* 1768, when the other ma-
' riners were paid and difcharged, he
' was ftill detained on board againft his
' will.

' HERE he continued for fome time, till
' he contrived to give the officers the flip,
' and by the affiftance and advice of fome
' friends, went to *Doctors Commons*, and ap-
' plied to Mr. *Faulckner*, a proctor, to put
' him in a way of recovering his wages, or
' fome other recompence for his labour.
' Mr. *Faulckner* accordingly wrote to
' *Arthur Jones*, one of the owners, for
' that purpofe; and *Rogers* being ap-
' pointed likewife to meet *Jones* at the
' proctor's office, was waiting at a pub-
' lic houfe, in *Doctors Commons*, till fent
' for; when *Jones*, *Seffins*, and another
' man, came into the houfe, forced *Ro-*
                                    ' *gers*

‘ *gers* into a coach, conveyed him back,
‘ and forced him on board another ship,
‘ where he was chained to the main-
‘ maſt, till he was releaſed by the deputy-
‘ marſhal of the High Court of Admiralty,
‘ with the aſſiſtance of Mr. *Shea*, one of his
‘ old maſters, and ſome other friends, who
‘ had obtained a warrant to take him out of
‘ his confinement.

‘ SEVERAL reaſons prevented his ap-
‘ plying for redreſs of theſe injuries,
‘ till the beginning of the year 1774,
‘ when Mr. *Torriano* was employed to
‘ commence an action againſt *Arthur*
‘ *Jones*, as one of the owners, for the
‘ purpoſe of recovering the uſual wages,
‘ or ſome other recompence in lieu there-
‘ of.

‘ AFTER the uſual proceedings, the
‘ cauſe was brought for hearing on June,
‘ 29, 1776; when the facts being all
‘ clearly proved as above ſtated, the prin-
‘ cipal queſtion was,——*How far the plea*
‘ *of SLAVERY, ſet up by the defendant,*
‘ *could be admitted in bar of the demand of*
‘ *wages?*

‘ IT was inſiſted on by the counſel on be-
‘ half of *Rogers*, that the kind of ſlavery,
‘ here ſpoken of, never had any exiſtence
‘ under the laws of *England*; and in ſupport
‘ of that, referred to the well known Caſe
‘ of

' of *Knowles* and *Somerset*, before lord
' *Mansfield*; and likewise to a late one
' in the PREROGATIVE COURT, of *Cay* and
' *Crichton*.

' THE counsel for the defendant argu-
' ed, that, till the case of *Somerset*, the
' law of *England* admitted slavery; and
' in support of this, they quoted the au-
' thority of Lord Chief Justice *Hale*; and,
' in particular, the opinions of the Lords
' *Talbot* and *Hardwick*.'

THE Decree of the Court thereupon was, in substance, as follows.

' *THERE are two principal points in*
' *this cause*; (said the Judge)
' 1st. *Whether such a service is proved (as*
' *stated in the summary Petition) as to enti-*
' *tle the plaintiff to the wages demanded? and*
' 2dly. *Whether the plea of slavery shall be*
' *a sufficient bar to the claim?*
' *With regard to the* FIRST, *it appears by*
' *the fullest evidence, that the plaintiff had serv-*
' *ed on board the ship, either in the capacity*
' *of assistant to the* COOK, *or as cook himself,*
' *during the greatest part of the voyage, and*
' *consequently was entitled to some recompence*
' *for his services*; *but not being entered as a*
' *mariner in the ship's books, nor having any*
                                    ' *stipulated*

'stipulated wages affigned him, it being proba-
' ble that the owners meant to fell him again in
' the Weft Indies, he cannot be allowed any spe-
' cific fum under the name of WAGES; but as
' he certainly performed the duty to which he
' was affigned, without any objection to his be-
' haviour in it, the maritime law clearly gives
' him a QUANTUM MERUIT. The cook's
' wages appear to have been £1. 5s. 6d. per
' Month, which is more than Rogers, moft
' probably, cou.d fairly deferve. But upon in-
' spection of the mariners contract, it appears
' that there were several negroe boys in the
' same ship, in the quality of apprentices, who
' were allowed from 10s. to 17s. and 6d. per
' month;' he signified his opinion therefore,
that Rogers might fairly deferve 15s. per
month, which he accordingly decreed him,
from the time of his being firft carried on
board.

' With regard to the SECOND point, it was
' urged (faid the judge) that the plaintiff was
' a SLAVE, and confequently was not entitled to
' any reward for his service at all.

' The practice of buying and selling slaves
' (the learned judge remarked) was cer-
' tainly very common in England, before
' the cafe of SOMERSET, in the Court of
' King's Bench, 1772, but however it might
' have been the law of the Royal Ex-
                                    ' change

APPENDIX, No. 11.

'*change,*' he hoped, '*it never was the law of England.*

'*The* OPINIONS *of lord* Hardwicke, *and lord* Talbot, *when Attorney and Solicitor general, have been quoted in support of this practice, and have formerly given too much countenance to it, though they seemed originally to have been only applied to the difference created by baptism.*'

'*But by a late determination of one of the ablest judges that ever presided in this kingdom, these opinions have been held to be mistaken and unsound; and there can be no further doubt, that the claim of* SLAVERY *is not maintainable by the laws of* England.

'*The law therefore was the same before the time of the above opinions, as since; and, consequently, refers to all sales whatsoever of this nature; which are every one illegal: and therefore the pretended sale in the present case, in 1766, was an absolute nullity; and when the allegation, stating the sale, was admitted on behalf of the owners, had* Rogers *appeared, under protest, upon this point of law, it would have been received in bar of the plea!*

'*The owners seem to have acted upon a mistaken notion of their right; but as the claim of slavery is clearly against the law of this country, and as it appeared that* Rogers
'*had*

' *had always acted in some useful capacity dur-*
' *ing the whole time of his having been on*
' *board,*' the judge said, he thought ' *him*
' *entitled to a* QUANTUM MERUIT *for his*
' *service,*'———which he accordingly fixed as
above; and condemned the owners in costs;
which were immediately taxed to the amount
of £81. 11s. 0d.

APPEN-

[87]

APPENDIX,

(No. 12.)

From the General Evening Post, No. 6033. *June* 13th, 1772.

To the Editor of the General Evening Post.

SIR,

AS the great cause depending between Mr. *Stuart*, and *Somerset*, the negro, is at present one of the principal topics of general conversation, by inserting the following you will afford a seasonable and rational entertainment to your readers. I am your's, &c.

Extract of a letter from a person in Maryland, *to his friend in* Philadelphia.

' I am so happy as to think as you do,
' with regard to trading in man, or keep-
' ing

'ing him a slave. The custom is wicked
'and iniquitous, neither consistent with
'reason, or the laws of God or man.
'Poor unhappy slaves, particularly those
'forced from their places of nativity, are
'most certainly deplorable objects of com-
'miseration. I never bought more than
'two during twenty years residence here.
'One proved to be the son of an African
'Prince; he was a most comely youth: hav-
'ing observed his uncommon good parts,
'I sent him to school, and used him like
'a free man during his stay with me. The
'directors of the African Company having
'enquired, and offered a reward for him,
'I by a public act presented the poor crea-
'ture with his freedom, gave him an order
'for the reward aforesaid, and sent him to
'London; from whence the following year
'he remitted me the same sum he cost me,
'and sundry rich goods to the amount of
'three hundred pounds and upwards, and
'therewith a letter in his own native lan-
'guage, translated by Dr. Desaguillier, of
'Cambridge.

'The next I purchased was an unhap-
'py lad, kidnapped from his free pa-
'rents at the taking of Guadaloupe.
'During his stay with me he decayed or
'pined so much, and expressed so sensible
'a sorrow of cruel separation from his
'aged

'aged parents, relations, and countrymen,
' that actuated by the unerring good provi-
' dence which directs us in all our good deeds,
' I likewife fet this poor creature free, and
' fent him to his native place. Providence
' again would not excufe my being further
' rewarded, for performing this my duty
' as a Chriftian. The truly honeft father,
' from the produce of his plantations, has
' made me prefents to the amount of fifty
' pounds fterling, with direction to draw
' upon him for the full coft of the poor
' youth, which I do never intend, being
' more than paid by prefents

'I write this to convince you that the in-
' habitants of Africa are not fuch fenfelefs
' brutifh creatures as thoughtlefs authors
' reprefent them to be: they undoubtedly
' are capable of receiving inftruction, and
' far out-do Chriftians in many commend-
' able virtues. Poor creatures! their great-
' eft unhappinefs is being acquainted with
' *Chriftians*. ‡

‡ The worthy and benevolent writer muft mean fuch *Chriftians* only as thofe, who carry out with them nothing of that moft amiable profeffion of religion but *the name*, to the '*ſhip wrack*.' of their own fouls, and to the difgrace of their native country, if that alfo is called *Chriftian!*

'The following is a letter from the
'Negro Prince, some time after he
'arrived at *London*, to his master
'in *Maryland*. Translated by Dr.
'*Desaguillier*, of *Cambridge*, 1743.

From the great city, 3d moon after my release.

' O my kind merciful master, my good
' white brother, too good, a very good son of
' a good woman, and of a very good old
' man, created good old people by the GREAT
' SPIRIT, who made my country, thy poor
' (I should say heretofore poor) most grate-
' ful black prisoner, now rendered rich by
' thy goodness and mercy, is now most
' dead, most drunk, most mad with joy!
' Why is he so? because he is going to his
' good warm country, to his good old mo-
' ther, to his good old father, to his little
' sister and his brother. In my good warm
' country all things are good, except the
' white people who live there, and come in
' flying-houses to take away poor black priso-
' ners from their mothers, their fathers, their
' sisters and brothers, to kill them with hun-
' ger and filth, in the cellars of their flying-
' houses, wherein if they do not die fast
' enough,

'enough, and poor prisoners talk for bread
'and water, and want to feel the wind,
'and to see THE GREAT SPIRIT, to com-
'plain to him, to tell him all, or to see the
'trees of his good warm country once
'more for the last time, the King of the
'white people [*probably the negro meant
'the captain*] orders the officer called Jack,
'to kill many of the black prisoners, with
'whips, with ropes, knives, axes and salt.
'The governor of thy flying-house has
'been to shew that which is to carry me and
'him to my good warm country; I am
'glad, very glad indeed! He goes there
'with wine Should he be sick, (and white
'people seldom escape being so there,) be-
'cause of thee my kind merciful master,
'and good white brother, and because he
'has been good to me, and is a very good
'white man too, I will nurse him myself,
'my mother, my father, my little sister,
'and my brother, shall be his brother, his
'mother, his father, and his sister too;
'he shall have one large heap of ele-
'phants teeth and gold, for thee my kind
'merciful master, and kind brother, and
'one for himself also (but smaller.) He at
'present is my father, I eat at his house,
'and lie there too upon the bed thou pre-
'sented me with. His woman is my mo-
'ther,

' ther, and kindly nurfes me, being very
' fick of the fea and fire made of black
' ftones. I have received a great quantity
' of gold, befides what thou did prefent
' me with by means of thy hand writing,
' to the people who are to fend me to my
' country, fome part whereof I have given
' to the governor of thy fwimming-houfe,
' to be fent to thee; had I an houfeful
' fhould fend the whole with equal plea-
' fure; however, thou fhalt fee hereafter,
' that black people are not beafts, and do
' know how to be grateful. After thou my
' kind merciful mafter and good white bro-
' ther left me in thy fwiming houfe, we,
' thy white people, and we thy grateful black
' prifoners, were by the GREAT SPIRIT, who
' was angry with us, fent by the wind into
' an immenfe great river, where we had like
' to have been drowned, and where we could
' fee neither fun nor moon, for fix days and
' nights. I was dying during one who'e
' moon, the governor was my father, and
' gave me thofe good things thou prefented
' me with on my bed, he lodged me in the
' little room thy carpenter built for me.
' Thou gave me more cloaths than I could
' carry, yet I was very cold; nothing avail-
' ed with poor black prifoner, till at laft hav-
' ing THE GREAT SPIRIT to fend me fafe to
' thy houfe on fhore, I thought I was carried
                                        ' there,

* there, [*this appears to have been a dream*]
' where thou my good white brother did ufe
' me with wonted goodnefs, fpake to THE
',GREAT SPIRIT, and TO HIS SON, that I
' might keep fo during the voyage and af-
' terwards, which they have done for thy
' fake; they will always do me good becaufe
' of thee my good white brother; therefore
' my kind merciful mafter, do not forget thy
' poor black prifoner. When thou doft fpeak
' to THE GREAT SPIRIT and TO HIS SON, I
' do know he will hear thee, I fhall never
' be fick more, for which I fhall be thank-
' ful. Pray fpeak for my good old mother,
' my good father, my little fifter, and my
' brother; I wifh they may be healthy, to
' many very many moons, as many as the
' hairs on thy head; I love them all much, yet
' I think not fo much as I do thee, I could die
' in my country for thee, could I do thee any
' kindnefs. Indeed THE GREAT SPIRIT well
' knows I mean no lie, fhall always fpeak to
' him for thy good, believe me my good
' white brother, thy poor black prifoner is
' not a liar.

Dgiagola, fon of Dgiagola, Prince of Foat, ‖ *Africa.*

¶ The country, here called FOAT, is probably named (the found being nearly the fame) from PHUT, the
third fon of *Ham*; concerning whom, and his defcendants

94 APPENDIX, No. 12.

scendants in the interior part of *Africa*, particular mention is made in Mr. *Bryant*'s letter, on the descent of the negroes. See Appendix, No. 4 pages 48 to 52: or perhaps it may mean '*the very country upon the ri-* ' *ver Gambia on one side,*' which (as Mr *Bryant* informs us from *Bluet*) ' *is at this day called* PHUTA.' See p. 50.

INDEX

OF

Texts referred to in the foregoing Work.

GENESIS.

Chap.	Verses.	Pages.
ix.	28.	47 n.
x.	5, 6.	App. 48.

EXODUS.

xxi.	2.	57 n.
	5, 6.	15.
xxiii.	9.	7, 41.
xxxiv.	11, 12.	4 n.

LEVITICUS.

xviii.		4, 12.
xix.	18.	App. 24.
	33, 34.	6, 9, 42.
xxv.	44 to 46.	3, 26. 65.
	39 to 43.	16.
	39 to 46.	App. 18, 25.

NUMBERS.

xxxi.	17.	11 n.
xxxiii.	55, 56.	12 n.

DEU-

Deuteronomy.

Chap.	Verses.	Pages.
vii.	1.	8.
	2.	11 n.
	16.	5, 11 n.
	23, 24.	5 n.
ix.	5.	12 n.
x.	17 to 19.	6, 43.
xv.	3.	App. 23.
	12.	56.
	12 to 14.	63.
	15.	7.
	18.	65.
xx.	16.	10 n.
xxiii.	15, 16.	49, 54.
	19.	App. 23.
xxv.	19.	11.

II Chronicles.

xiv.	9.	22 n.
xvi.	8.	22.

Job.

xxxi	38 to 40.	60, 61.

Psalms.

lxviii.	31.	22, 24.

Proverbs.

xiv.	34.	App. 15.

Jeremiah.

xiii.	23.	App. 44.
xxii.	13.	60.
xxxi.	29.	App. 11.

Ezekiel.

xviii.	3, 4, 20.	App. 11.

[97]

Amos.

Chap.	Verses.	Pages.
viii.	7, 8.	15 n.

Habakkuk.

| i. | 13. | App. 15. |
| iii. | 7. | App. 52. |

Ecclesiasticus.

| xxxiv. | 22. | 61. |

Matthew.

v.	44, 45.	39.
vii.	12.	42, 45.
		App. 8.
	23.	67.
xix.	8, 9.	App. 22.
xxiv.	30.	21.
xxv.	34 to 46.	37, 38.
	40.	21, 67.
	12.	67.
xxviii.	19.	18.

Luke.

| iv. | 18. | App. 14. |
| x. | 7. | 59. |

Acts.

viii.	27, 28.	24.
	27.	App. 11.
x.	34.	App. 11.

Romans.

| viii. | 17. | 20. |

I Corinthians.

iii.	16, 17.	19.
vi.	19, 20.	19.
vii.	22, 23.	App. 35, 36.

Gala-

GALATIANS.

Chap.	Verses.	Pages.
iv.	5, 6, 7.	19.
v.	14.	42.

EPHESIANS.

iii.	6.	19.

COLOSSIANS.

iv.	1.	62.
	7, 9.	App. 35.

I THESSALONIANS.

iii.	13.	21.

PHILEMON.

The Intention of the whole Epistle considered as far as it relates to Onesimus. } App. 31 to 38.

JAMES.

v.	3, 4.	58.

II PETER.

i.	3, 4.	20.

JUDE.

xiv.	15.	21.

REVELATIONS.

i.	7.	21.
xiv.	6.	41.

INDEX.

INDEX.

A.

ADMIRALTY, report of a Determination againſt *Slavery* in the Admiralty Court before Sir George Hay, in the Caſe of *Rogers*, alias *Rigges*, againſt *Jones*, *App.* 75. 79.

Africa, the Goſpel of Chriſt received there earlier than in Europe, 21. The antiquity and purity of the church of Habaſſinia, 23. Early councils aſſembled there, 24. Lamentable apoſtaſy of the African church, the cauſe of the preſent barbarous ignorance which now prevails there, 26. This Example cited by Abp. Sharp as a Warning to Britain, 44, *note*. All the inhabitants of, aſſuredly the deſcendants of Ham, *App.* 48.

African Merchant, the juſtification of ſlavery from the Moſaic law, by a writer under that name, examined, 3. Prince, letter from, to his maſter in Maryland, *App.* 90.

Africans, their deſcent inquired into, 48. See *Negroes*.

America, a propoſal for the gradual enfranchiſement of negro ſlaves there, *App.* 57.

Ariſtotle, his argument in juſtification of ſlavery refuted, 27, *note*.

B.

Barbadoes, the killing of negroes there, only punished by a fine, 33.
Beattie, Dr. his examination of Aristotle on the subject of slavery, and of Mr. Hume on the mental inferiority of negroes, 27, *note*.
Benevolence, universal, the distinguishing characteristic of Christianity, *App.* 28.
Bishops, numerous Assemblies of them in the Ecclesiastical Synods of Africa, 24, 25.
Blackwell, Dr. his definition of liberty, *App.* 13.
Bond-servants among the Israelites, who might legally be made so, 3. The law of, repealed by the Gospel, 46.
Brethren, all mankind connected under the idea of, by our Christian obligations, 40. It is inconsistent with Christianity that any of them should be slaves, *App.* 33.
Bryant, Mr. his letter to the Author concerning the descent of the negroes, *App.* 47.

C.

Canaan, falsely reputed the Father of the African negroes, 47, 48.
Candid Reflections upon the Judgement lately awarded by the Court of King's Bench, &c. on the Negroe Cause. The Author of a Book so entitled, convicted of *uncandid Reflections*, *App.* 69 to 71.
Cave, Dr. his Account of the great Ecclesiastical Synods in Africa cited, 24, 25.
Cay and Crichton, report of the case of, in the Prerogative Court, *App.* 77.
Charity, Christian, is not to be partial in its objects, *App.* 28.

Christianity,

Christianity, the benevolent spirit of, totally inconsistent with the tyrannical claims of slaveholding, 17. Negroes, as well as the rest of mankind, included under the Gospel dispensation, 19. Connects all the human race under the idea of brethren, 40. None of the Levitical laws can justify slavery under, 41.
Chusim, the usual Name for *Negroes* in the Old Testament, 22. See also Letters on the Descent of the Negroes, *App.* 44. 47.
Congress, American, their prohibition of the importation of slaves, should be followed by the gradual emancipation of those now in the country, *App.* 56.
Councils, Christian, a list of those held in Africa during the third and fourth centuries, 24.

D.

Dgiagola, Prince of *Foat*, released from Slavery by his Master in Maryland, *App.* 88. His grateful Letter for that favour translated by Dr. Desaguillier, *App.* 90.
Desaguillier, see above.

E.

Elegy on the miserable state of an African slave, by Mr. Shenstone, *App.* 39.
Emancipation of slaves, in the Colonies, a comparative view of the different modes of, *App.* 16. This work remains to be done by the American Congress, *App.* 56.
Estwick, Mr. his report of the late Judgement in the Court of King's Bench by Lord Mansfield, in the Case of *Somerset* and *Knowles*, *App.* 65. His own Remarks thereupon, *App.* 69. Answered by other Remarks on that Judgement, *App.* 72.

Ethiopians,

Ethiopians, received the Chriſtian faith before the Europeans, 21. Their defcent traced, 22, *note*.

F.

Fcat, a Region in Africa, probably the fame that is called *Phuta* from *Phut* the Son of Ham, *App.* 93.

H.

Habaſſinia, Church of, remains a Monument of Chriſtianity among the Sons of Ham, 23.
Habeas Corpus Act. Severity thereof againſt thofe who attempt to carry away any perfon by force out of this Kingdom, *App.* 76.
Ham, the common father of all the inhabitants of Africa, *App.* 48.
Havanna, regulations adopted by the Spaniards there, for the gradual enfranchiſement of negroes, *App.* 54.
Hay, Sir George. See Admiralty and Prerogative Court.
Heathen, under the Mofaic law, who were implied by that term, 3. Were devoted to deſtruction for their abominable vices, 4. Diſtinguiſhed from *ſtrangers*, 5. The bondage they were doomed to, not to be extended to ſtrangers at large, 9. Are by no means excluded from the benevolence of Chriſtians, 39.
Hume, Mr. his opinion of the mental inferiority of Negroes, controverted by Dr. Beattie, 28, *note*.

I.

Jews, were by the Mofaic law permitt_d to make bond fervants or flaves of the Heathen, 3. And
why,

why, 4. Were commanded to treat ſtrangers kindly, 6. Over whom their legal power of bondage extended, 8. Their national privileges not to be claimed by any other people, 10. The limitations under which they might hold their brethren in bondage, 14. Such bond brethren were to be generouſly aſſiſted on difmiſſion, 56. Their conſtitutions not ſtrictly confiſtent with the law of nature as aſſerted by Mr. Thompſon, *App.* 19. Inſtances of contrariety, *App.* 21. Infidelity of the preſent age, ſo many proofs of our growing apoſtaſy from the Chriſtian Religion, 26, *note.*

K.

King's Bench, report of a Determination in that Court before Lord Mansfield *againſt Slavery*, in the Caſe of *Somerſet* and *Knowles*, or *Stewart*, *App.* 65. Remarks on that Determination, ditto 69. A Defence of, ditto, ditto, 72.

L.

Labourer always worthy of his hire, 59.
Law of England, both common and ſtatute, not to contradict the laws of God, 55.
Letter, from an African prince to his maſter in Maryland, *App.* 90.
Liberty, the univerſality of, aſſerted by Mr. Otis, *App.* 9. Definition of, *App.* 13.
Lutholf, his account of the antiquity and purity of the church of Habaſſinia cited, 23, *note.*

M.

Mansfield, Lord, the ſubſtance of his ſpeech in the caſe of Somerſet and Knowles, *App.* 65. Remarks on it, *App.* 69. See King's Bench Court.

Maryland,

Maryland, account of the cruel treatment of the negroes and convict flaves there, *App.* 42.
Mafon and Jones, *App.* 80.
Mauritania, how firft peopled, *App.* 49.
Mercator, the pleas in behalf of flavery by the writer under this title, refuted, 47.
Monthly Review, confiderations on negroe flavery extracted from, 3.
Morgan, Mr. extract from his Plan for the abolition of flavery in the Weft Indies, *App.* 62.
Mofaic law, how far, and on what account, flavery was tolerated under it, 3. The benevolent treatment of ftrangers ftrongly inculcated by, 6. Will not juftify flavery under the Chriftian difpenfation, 41. Is fuperfeded by it, 46. Not ftrictly confiftent with the law of nature, as afferted by Mr. Thompfon, *App.* 19. Inftances of contrariety, *App.* 21.

N.

Negroes, the enflaving of, not to be juftified from the Mofaic law, 8. Are branded by their mafters with hot irons, 15, *note*. Are equally intitled to the promifes of God in the Gofpel, with the reft of mankind, 19. Received the Chriftian faith before the Europeans, 21. Dr. Beattie's defence of, againft the infinuations of Mr. Hume, 28, *note*. Their murder compounded for by money in Barbadoes, 33. One advertifed for in London, and defcribed by a brafs collar like a dog, 35. Are not treated according to the Chriftian law of doing as we would be done by, 43. Are treated like cattle, 45. Not defcended from Canaan, 47, 48. alfo *App.* 12. Rewards offered by our Colony laws for killing them when they run away, 50. Their different treatment in England and America inconfiftent with reafon, law, and religion, *App.* 7.

7. Ought to be emancipated, *App.* 12. Examination into the moſt prudent means of emancipation, *App.* 16. Their cruel treatment in Maryland, *App.* 42. Queries reſpecting the deſcent of them, *App.* 44. Reply to, *App.* 47. Regulations adopted by the Spaniards for the enfranchiſement of, *App.* 54. A Propoſal for the gradual enfranchiſement of the Britiſh American ſlaves, *App.* 57. May thus be converted into free peaſants, *App.* 60. Natural tendency of our retaining them in ſlavery, *App.* 62. Remarks on the judgement of the Court of King's Bench in the caſe of Somerſet, *App.* 72.
Neighbours, all mankind intitled to be eſteemed ſo, under the Chriſtian diſpenſation, 40.

O.

Oneſimus, in what ſenſe he was recommended back to his former maſter Philemon by St. Paul, *App.* 31. Was then a miniſter of the Goſpel, *App.* 34, *note.* Became biſhop of Epheſus, *App.* 37, *note.*
Otis, Mr. aſſerts the univerſality of liberty, *App.* 9.

P.

Paleſtine, the ſeven nations of, the only *ſtrangers* whom the Jews were permitted to hold in abſolute ſlavery, 8.
Paul, St. his Exhortation to Slaves to continue in the State in which they were called, affords no Argument for ſlavery, *App.* 6. Is vindicated from Mr. Thompſon's charge of juſtifying ſlavery, *App.* 31.
Philemon. St. Paul's Epiſtle to him conſidered, *App.* 31—38. See Oneſimus.

Planters,

Planters, American, their pleas for slavery invalidated, 59.
Prerogative Court, report of a Determination in that Court before Dr. Hay against Slavery, in the Case of Cay and Crichten, *App.* 75. 77.
Proposal by the Author for the gradual enfranchisement of negroe slaves in America, *App.* 57.

R.

Reports of Determinations in the several Courts of Law against *Slavery*, viz. King's Bench, *App.* 65. Admiralty Court, ditto 79. Prerogative Court, ditto 77.
Retribution, Law of, referred to, *App.* 30.
Rogers, alias Rigges, against Jones, report of the case of, in the high court of Admiralty, *App.* 79.

S.

Saracens, query relating to their descent, *App.* 50, *note*.
Servants, fugitive, how treated in the British Colonies, 50, 51. Comparison between their case and that of negroe slaves, 52, *note*.
Sharp, Abp. his warning to England by the example of God's Judgements against the Africans, 44, *note*.
Shenstone, Mr. his elegy on the miserable state of an African slave, *App.* 39.
Slavery, is not to be justified by any of the Levitical laws under the Christian dispensation, 41. Considerations on, from the Monthly Review, *App.* 3. No positive law in favour of, either in England or America, *App.* 8.
Slaves, who might legally be made so by the Israelites, 3. Are branded with hot irons in the
British

British plantations, 15, *note*. The killing of them compounded for by act of assembly at Barbadoes, 33. One advertised for and described by a brass collar like a dog. 35. The holders of, cannot be real christians, 38. How treated on running away, by our American laws, 50. Examination into the most prudent means of emancipating, *App*. 16.

Somerset and *Knowles*, Case of, see King's Bench.

Spaniards, regulations adopted by, for the gradual enfranchisement of negroes, *App*. 54.

Strangers, benevolence toward, strongly enjoined by the Mosaic law, 6. 41. The parable of the good Samaritan teaches Christians to consider all men as neighbours, *App*. 24.

T.

Theophylact, Abp. his plea for slavery on the authority of St. Paul, refuted, *App*. 32, *note*.

Thompson, Rev. Mr. examination of his defence of the negroe slave trade, *App*. 18.

W.

Wages, always due for labour, 59. Are decreed by the high court of Admiralty to a negroe slave, *App*. 83.

F I N I S.

By the same AUTHOR.

Printed for B. WHITE, at Horace's Head, in Fleet-Street.

I. A Short Treatise on the English Tongue. Being an Attempt to render the Reading and Pronunciation of the same more easy to Foreigners. 1767.

II. Remarks on several very important Prophecies. 1st Edition 1768. 2d Edition 1775.

III. A Representation of the Injustice and dangerous Tendency of Tolerating Slavery; or of admitting the least Claim of Private Property in the Persons of Men *in England*. Being in Answer to an Opinion given in the Year 1729, by the (then) Attorney General and Solicitor General concerning the Case of Slaves in *Great Britain*. 1769.

IV. Remarks concerning the Encroachments on the River Thames near *Durham Yard*. 1771.

V. An Appendix to the Representation of the Injustice and dangerous Tendency of *Tolerating Slavery*, &c. 1772.

VI. Remarks on the Opinions of some of the most celebrated Writers on CROWN LAW, respecting the due Distinction between *Manslaughter* and *Murder*. 1773.

VII. In Two Parts. 1. A Declaration of the Peoples *Natural Right* to a Share in the Legislature; which is the fundamental Principle of *the British Constitution of State*. 2. A Declaration, or Defence of the same *Doctrine*, when applied *particularly to* THE PEOPLE OF IRELAND. 1774.

The following TRACTS *by the fame* AUTHOR,

Printed for B. WHITE, at Horace's Head, Fleet-Street, and E. and C. DILLY in the Poultry.

VIII. *The Law of paſſive Obedience*; or, Chriſtian Submiſſion to perſonal Injuries.—Wherein is ſhewn that the ſeveral Texts of Scripture which command the entire Submiſſion of *Servants* or *Slaves* to their *Maſters*, cannot authorize the latter to exact an *involuntary Servitude:* and alſo that the ſeveral Texts which enjoin *Submiſſion* to *Rulers* and *Magiſtrates*, do not juſtify the dangerous Doctrine of un *unlimited paſſive Obedience.* 1776.

IX. " *The Law of Liberty*;" or (as it is called in Scripture *by way of eminence*) " the *Royal Law*," by which *all Mankind* will certainly *be judged!* 1776.

X. The Law of Retribution; or a ſerious Warning to *Great Britain* and her *Colonies*, founded on unqueſtionable Examples of GOD's temporal Vengeance againſt Tyrants, Slave-holders, and Oppreſſors. The Examples are ſelected from Predictions in the Old Teſtament of *national* Judgements, which (being compared with their actual Accompliſhment) demonſtrate " the ſure Word of Prophecy," as well as the immediate Interpoſition of divine Providence, to recompence impenitent *Nations* according to their Works. 1776.

Now in the Preſs for Publication, by B. WHITE, in Fleet-Street, and E. and C. DILLY, in the Poultry.

I. A Tract *on the Law of Nature*, and Principles of Action in Man.

II THE CASE OF SAUL; being an Appendage to the former Tract, wherein the *compound Nature* and various *Principles of Action in* MAN (with the Reality of *ſupernatural, ſpiritual Influence*, both *good* and *bad*) are proved by unqueſtionable Examples from the Hiſtory of that unfortunate Monarch, and alſo from many other parts of Scripture.

www.ingramcontent.com/pod-product-compliance
Lightning Source LLC
Chambersburg PA
CBHW020829190426
43197CB00037B/894